TV SCENES
for
ACTORS

Selected Short Scenes from
"The Golden Age of T.V. Drama"

BY

SIGMUND A. STOLER

MERIWETHER PUBLISHING LTD.
COLORADO SPRINGS, COLORADO

Meriwether Publishing Ltd., Publisher
P.O. Box 7710
Colorado Springs, CO 80933

Editor: Arthur Zapel
Typesetting: Sharon Garlock
Cover design: Michelle Z. Gallardo

© Copyright MCMLXXXIX Meriwether Publishing Ltd.
Printed in the United States of America
First Edition

Library of Congress Cataloging-in-Publication Data

Stoler, Sigmund A.
    TV scenes for actors : selected short scenes from "The golden age of TV drama" / by Sigmund A. Stoler : foreword by Cliff Robertson.
        p.   cm.
    ISBN 0-916260-61-5
    1. Acting for television. 2. Television plays, American.
I. Title.
PN1992.8.A3S76   1989
791.45'028--dc20
                                               89-12942
                                                 CIP

To Betty — for caring.

Cliff Robertson

Journalist, writer, actor Cliff Robertson has had a varied career. He has been acclaimed for many successes on Broadway and in a long list of noteworthy motion pictures. He has won the Academy Award, an Emmy Award and a Theatre World Award — the big three of film, TV and Broadway acting honors. He also has been active with numerous charitable organizations having served as the 1984 National Chairman of the American Cancer Society. He has recently been honored by the Screen Actors Guild for his work in exposing corrupt forces in Hollywood.

FOREWORD
THE GOLDEN YEARS OF TELEVISION

The television "Golden Years" (roughly 1950-1965) has to me been a contradicition in terms. While there was certainly the excitement of a "new age in communication," there were also obstacles aplenty. Not atypical of any new frontier, be it the Industrial Revolution, the Automotive Age, or, God help us, the Age of the Atom (shades of Three Mile Harbor and Chernobyl); every bold step forward for mankind is invariably followed by a stumble or two.

Witness smoke-choked cities of the Victorian and Automotive Ages and today's hazards of radiation. Although the "Golden Years" of television had none of those lethal hazards, they *did* have hazards. Some, in retrospect, amusing — some disastrous! I can recall a few:

In the mid-fifties, NBC aired a weekly dramatic hour titled, "Robert Montgomery Presents." For those too young to know, Robert Montgomery had been a rather elegant leading man in Hollywood in the 30's and 40's. His acting talent was formidable. I still recall vividly his chilling performance in "Night Must Fall." To this day every time I hear the plaintive melody, "Mighty Like a Rose," I remember running home from a Saturday night movie at the Granada Theatre in La Jolla, California, certain that the homicidal killer was lurking behind every palm tree ready to devour my seven-year-old body.

Mr. Montgomery was the producer of this NBC top dramatic show. He also was the proud paternal producer of Elizabeth Montgomery, star of the long-running "Bewitched" TV series of the 60's.

And she was, incidentally, the "ingenue" to my "juvenile" in my first Broadway play, "Late Love." Elizabeth and I played in some of her father's shows. In fact, in the summer of 1953, I was a "regular" in his live summer series. Working as a "regular" made for some interesting experiences. I remember one that still shakes me.

I was the "juvenile" in a murder mystery with quite a large role. In this one scene in the third act, I confronted a suspect with (I thought) great dramatic force. It was an "eyeball to eyeball" J'accuse confrontation or at least it was *supposed* to be. To my great consternation, the young lady could not keep her eyes *on* me. No matter how forcefully I stared, nor how angrily I spoke, she continually averted my gaze, glancing downward. Even when she spoke, she looked downward.

At this point, I was convinced I had intimidated the poor actress with the dramatic force of my talent. As she continued to lower her head an interesting thing began to happen. My dramatic "force" began to abate, my impassioned anger to drift away, my voice softened. I was developing an "understanding" for the accused. In true fidelity to my actor's studio training, I was "adjusting." Adjusting, hell! I was feeling sorry for the girl! Sorry for a homicidal murderer who had just carved up her family with a 12" kitchen knife! She, poor soul, continued to drop her head downward, occasionally glancing up at me with a sense of increasing panic. I increased my "adjustment," my sympathy, my tenderness. I was giving way to a tidal wave of warmth and, yes, love! My Actors Studio mentors, Lee Strassberg, Harold Clurman and Elia Kazan were whispering in my sub-conscious — "Go with it, give in to her sorrow, go with the flow."

I went all the way! Tears began to fall down my young cheeks. I tried to hold back, my speech faltered, my breath shortened. I was *weeping* for Christ's sake! She was completely stunned and addled by my "adjustment." I continued to crumble, reaching out to her. I drew her resisting body to my chest. Continuing my J'accuse dialogue, I patted her like a frightened puppy. Her eyes no longer gazed downward, but straight ahead at the camera, wide-glazed and unbelieving! She could speak no more. She was in shock.

Sensing her condition, I continued my last speech with funereal compassion. My strange contrapuntal behavior accompanied my dialogue . . . "and with Satanic relish you plunged the 12-inch stainless steel butcher blade 10 inches into your grandmother's breast, twisted it six times, then proceeded to carve up the rest of the family like a Christmas goose!" I wept disconsolately as *she* led *me* away. Tragedy and fear stained my face — wild-eyed fear and panic on hers.

After the show:

DIRECTOR: What in God's name were you *doing* out there, Robertson?

ME: I was . . . I was . . .

DIRECTOR: You were *what?*

ME: I was reacting . . .

DIRECTOR: To *what* for Christ's sake!!?

ME: Her sorrow . . .

DIRECTOR: *What* sorrow? She's a killer for Christ's sake!

ME: It was . . . It was . . .

DIRECTOR: WHAT?!

ME: An "adjustment" . . .

DIRECTOR: An adjustment . . .?

ME: To her behavior — she couldn't hold my gaze. She looked away — downward — always downward.

DIRECTOR: That's right, Robertson. She *was* looking downward. Do you know *why* she kept looking downward?

ME: Her contrition, her remorse, her grief . . .

DIRECTOR: Her grief my ass! She was trying to signal you!

ME: Signal me?

DIRECTOR: Yeah! Your fly was open — wide open!

Not all our TV obstacles were in front of the camera. There was a high state of anxiety behind the lens as well. Floor managers were literally pulling actors to their next mark or set. Actors were skipping over cables *everywhere*. Wardrobe people were changing actors' costumes on the run. And the ever-present horror of crossing in *front* of a live camera — particularly humiliating during a murder or hospital operation scene — I mean, what do you say to the killer or doctor — "Excuuuuuse me?"

The Golden Years were, however, fruitful, a spawning place for people like Paddy Chayefsky, J. P. Miller, Horton Foote and Reginald Rose — directors like Sidney Lumet, John Frankenheimer, Arthur Penn, Daniel Petrie — and actors, of course, like Kim Stanley (probably the most gifted American actress since Laurette Taylor), Maureen Stapleton, Grace Kelly, Rod Steiger, Paul Newman, and the late James Dean to name but a few. A very few!

Yes, the Golden Years of television minted a treasury of talent. Television today, with all its high-tech embellishments, its dazzling pyrotechnics, will never, *can* never, replace the raw, naked energy of the Golden Age. Television then was the new "Emperor" of media. It may have been naked, but no one said so, and if they had, who would have cared? Certainly not us. After all, we *were* working!

Cliff Robertson

ACKNOWLEDGMENT

Production photos in this book were photographed at the studios of International Media Systems through the courtesy of Paul Franklin, president/director.

CONTENTS BY CATEGORY

NOTE: Some scenes are listed in more than one category.

Suspense

Behind the Scenes
A Name for Death
Getting Started
Just a Song at Twilight
A Generous Allowance
Edge of Danger
The Circle Closes

All Women Casts

The Circle Closes
A Joyous Holiday

Two Character Scenes

Edge of Danger
The Brass Ring
The Circle Closes
The Road Back
A Sense of Honor

Strong Characterizations

A Sense of Honor
Edge of Danger
A Name for Death
A Short Trip
A Joyous Holiday
Something Borrowed, Something Blue
Behind the Scenes
The Circle Closes
The Brass Ring
A Case of Mistaken Identity

Problem Scenes

Trade-Off
Out of the Tiger's Den
To See Ourselves
The Choice
Sudden Encounter
The Road Back
Trouble with the Third Party

Comedies

What's in a Name?
A Matter of Values
Finding the Right Key
Mama's Boy
A Case of Mistaken Identity
Allowance for Change
Something Borrowed, Something Blue
Watch Your Step
A Short Trip

TABLE OF CONTENTS

INTRODUCTION

In assembling this volume of short scenes taken from my television plays, the idea has been to give students an opportunity to work with material from the period in history now known as "The Golden Age of Television."

This was the time in the fifties and the early sixties when a truly large number of fine television plays were being presented. One of the shows that I wrote, "The Web," produced my Mark Goodson Productions (it was Goodson and Todman Productions then) was part of that period.

"The Web" was a complete half-hour mystery play that came on every Sunday night from 10 to 10:30 over CBS Television, and had a tremendous following because of its format. While the viewer knew who had done "the dirty deed", whatever that was, the suspense in the play was in learning how the "doer" was caught. The ultimate twist was that he (or she) was always snared in a web of his own making.

It was challenging, and a lot of work, to think of characters and new situations for these plays on a week-to-week basis. I hasten to add I did not write all of these shows. I was one of a stable of writers.

For this anthology, in the interest of variety since most of "The Web" plays involved murder, mayhem and worse, I have included scenes from some of my other not-so-violent series: "Appointment with Life," "Grand Central Station," and "Stars Over Hollywood," all produced over ABC and all in the same time period. To present current themes, I have written some original material.

Student actors studying and playing these scenes have an opportunity to do lines originally played by such famous actors as: Cliff Robertson, Jane Wyatt, Richard Widmark, Mercedes McCambridge, Leslie Wood, Lori March, Leora Dana, Frederic Worlock, Evelyn Varden, Berry Kroeger, and on and on and on. All the Broadway greats acted in plays of the era.

Now, as then, while television shows appear seamless, students will do well to remember there is never enough rehearsal time in television — at least there wasn't. The players have to work in very cramped quarters. While the camera can pull back to indicate depth, actors are really playing almost on top of each other. Staginess in acting is spotted immediately.

My experiences as a writer, while exhilarating, could also be frustrating and time-consuming. First, a proposal of what I planned to do had to be written in detail — eight to ten single-spaced typewritten pages. It was then re-written to accommodate endless suggested changes. Finally, an okay was given to write, but Gene Burr, the editor of "The Web" series, liked me to overwrite as it made one of his jobs easier, that of cutting the play to fit the time slots around the commercials.

At last, the script was set, the actors hired, and while I was allowed to watch the first run-through, and only the first, I wasn't allowed to talk. My job as a playwright was essentially over. I had no complaints. Some of the actors saw depths and nuances in my lines I never dreamed of, so by and large, I was pleased.

I must mention, however, I never really had an opportunity to know any of these glittering, glitzy, larger-than-life show people. Oh, I discussed near-sightedness with Jane Wyatt — we traded glasses; she is very near-sighted, worse than I am — and I spoke briefly about dieting with Mercedes McCambridge and Berry Kroeger, but that was about it.

This strictly-business attitude did not include Mark Goodson, head of Goodson Productions, New York and Hollywood, who was, and is, the head of the production company that produced my plays. He and I talked a great deal, became friends, and have remained friends to this day, I am pleased to say. It is only through his courtesy in allowing us to reproduce many of these selections that this collection became possible.

I want to wish good luck to all the actors who will be working with these scenes. It is understood that none of them can be presented professionally unless application is made to the author. This can be done by writing to:

Sigmund Stoler
7 Fairway Drive
Selinsgrove, PA 17810

Just a Song at Twilight

Cast of Characters

MILLIE HAMILTON

About 60, a fiercely energetic woman, capable, grey-haired, smartly dressed.

JENNIFER HALL

Age 24, very pretty with a liquid-speaking voice, sure of herself, outspoken, a realist.

TODD HAMILTON

Age 30, a thoroughly nice man, completely at ease with himself, good-looking, tolerant. He reflects the love he and Millie, his mother, have for each other.

1   *AT RISE:*   When the curtain opens, MILLIE HAMILTON is hanging
2   up a "Welcome Home, Todd" banner in the comfortable living
3   room of her home. There's a large bunch of balloons in one
4   corner, streamers hung about, and a general gala air about the
5   place. MILLIE is busy, busy, busy. She is well-dressed and is
6   hammering away when the door suddenly opens and TODD,
7   her son, bursts in with his girl friend, JENNIFER.
8

9   **TODD:**   *(Cries. Rushes to embrace MILLIE.)* **Mamma! Hey!**
10   **MILLIE:**   *(So glad to see him.)* **Hello, darling. Oh, Todd, you're**
11   **home.** *(Turns to JENNIFER.)* **And this is the fabulous girl**
12   **friend, Jennifer.**
13   **JENNIFER:**   **Hello, Mrs. Hamilton.**
14   **MILLIE:**   **Why, you're as pretty as you're supposed to be.**
15   **JENNIFER:**   **So are you.**
16   **MILLIE:**   *(Makes a deprecatory movement with her hand.)* **Just an**
17   **old crow, really — trying to keep up with things.**
18   **JENNIFER:**   **Tell that to someone else.**
19   **MILLIE:**   **Todd's told me all about you.**
20   **JENNIFER:**   **He's told me all about you. Your research at**
21   **Berryton's Community Hospital. He says you're famous and**
22   **you'll probably be nominated for a Nobel Science Prize.**
23   **MILLIE:**   **Oh, my stars. Todd exaggerates horribly. But maybe**
24   **you're used to it.**
25   **JENNIFER:**   **No.**
26   **TODD:**   **Mom, I never —**
27   **JENNIFER:**   **You see, I can never get by his good looks.**
28   **MILLIE:**   **Inherited from his father. Jerry is such a handsome**
29   **man. Every time I see him I think, why do men go on**
30   **looking absolutely gorgeous, and women just get wrinkly,**
31   **stooped and awful?**
32   **TODD:**   **Come on. You look the same to me as you did when I**
33   **was in the third grade.**
34   **MILLIE:**   **Oh, my dear.** *(Laughs)* **That's because you're**
35   **nearsighted and too vain to wear your glasses.**

1   JENNIFER: Well, I'd settle for looking like you when I'm
2   your age.
3   MILLIE: Oh, who cares anyway? Everybody fusses about
4   looks or being thin, and then forgets what the person's
5   really like. I mean, inside — where it really counts.
6   JENNIFER: That's what makes me color my hair.
7   MILLIE: I didn't know you did.
8   JENNIFER: Well, you know I work as a television anchor
9   woman on the news.
10 MILLIE: Todd told me.
11 JENNIFER: If you're not young, you'd better be young looking
12   or — *(Runs her finger over her throat as if her head would be*
13   *cut off.)*
14 MILLIE: That bad?
15 JENNIFER: Worse. Now, they'd like me to wear form-fitting
16   clothes. *(She laughs.)* Isn't it pathetic?
17 MILLIE: It sounds interesting though.
18 JENNIFER: It is. Not everyone I get to meet is important, but
19   he — or she — is interesting. I'll hand the job that.
20 MILLIE: Well, Jerry, my husband —
21 JENNIFER: *(Concerned)* Oh, Todd's told me.
22 MILLIE: He'd love to talk to you. Naturally, this had to be the
23   weekend he's making a speech someplace. On grocery
24   supermarkets. It's in Boston, I think. It never fails.
25 JENNIFER: He's in Boston?
26 MILLIE: I believe it's Boston. If it isn't, it's another large city.
27   I never see him. If he's not at the warehouse or his office,
28   he's inspecting the stores. But then there are fifty of them,
29   and they are in three states, and I'll admit it — it all takes
30   time.
31 JENNIFER: *(More puzzled.)* But, Mrs. Hamilton — *(Looks at*
32   *TODD.)* I thought —
33 MILLIE: Jerry learned long ago if he didn't supervise, things
34   could go downhill fast. Not that he can't delegate authority.
35   But to make the nitty-gritty decisions —

1   **JENNIFER:** But, Mrs. Hamilton —

2   **TODD:** *(Interrupting decisively)* **Mom, I think Jennifer's**

3   **pooped. Would you mind if she went to her room? We'll**

4   **be here the whole weekend. Dr. Slater is covering for me**

5   **in our group practice, so I don't have to worry about the**

6   **phone ringing.**

7   **MILLIE:** Well, Jennifer will be in your old room, darling.

8   **JENNIFER:** Oh, great.

9   **MILLIE:** *(To TODD)* **And you're in the guest room. Daddy and**

10   **I are in the same old bedroom. We're not about to change**

11   **at this stage of our lives.**

12   **JENNIFER:** Mrs. Hamilton, I'm a little confused. I thought —

13   **TODD:** *(Interrupting firmly)* **Oh, honey, you're not the only one**

14   **who's confused. Don't forget, we had a good ten-hour**

15   **drive from North Carolina. My eyes are still popping.**

16   **MILLIE:** Give me a minute, Jennifer, to check, will you? I'm

17   sure Todd's room is in good shape, but — *(She exits upstairs*

18   *at rear of set.)*

19   **TODD:** Take your time, Millie.

20   **MILLIE:** *(Stops. Calls back.)* **And don't call me Millie. I'm your**

21   **mother.** *(She disappears.)*

22   **TODD:** *(Laughs)* **Sit down a minute, love. You must be —**

23   **JENNIFER:** Todd, wait a minute. *(TODD looks up.)* **You told**

24   **me your father was dead.**

25   **TODD:** *(Conversationally)* **That's right.**

26   **JENNIFER:** *(Incredulous)* **That's right?**

27   **TODD:** It'll be a year next month.

28   **JENNIFER:** *(Frowns)* **Then what's your mother talking about?**

29   **He's at a seminar in Boston. Giving a speech.**

30   **TODD:** *(Calmly)* **I know.**

31   **JENNIFER:** *(Puts hands to forehead.)* **Wait a minute.** *(Pause.*

32   *Spaces out words.)* **Wait — a — minute. One of us has got**

33   **to be — or am I losing it?**

34   **TODD:** No.

35   **JENNIFER:** She knows he's dead?

1 TODD: Yes.

2 JENNIFER: I mean, dead and buried?

3 TODD: Yes.

4 JENNIFER: She's suffering from Alzheimer's disease?

5 TODD: She has a memory like a steel trap. How else could she

6   still be in research?

7 JENNIFER: You want to explain?

8 TODD: There's really nothing to explain, hon. She simply has

9   never accepted the fact that Dad died. To her, he's just

10   never around anymore. She doesn't see him. There's a

11   big difference in those two statements. Never around is

12   never around. She can live with that.

13 JENNIFER: But —

14 TODD: Who's she hurting if she pretends? We all delude

15   ourselves anyway, don't we? We feel like we're dying and

16   tell people we're fine. We get fired and say we quit. We

17   wear imitations and pretend they're real.

18 JENNIFER: Those things are one thing, but — life and death?

19   You sound as — far out as she is.

20 TODD: *(Somewhat stiffly.)* Hold it, honey. I don't consider my

21   mother far out.

22 JENNIFER: You encourage her in this belief?

23 TODD: I don't encourage or discourage her. Why should I?

24   She wouldn't believe me, and it would just make her

25   unhappy.

26 JENNIFER: The woman's in research. She works with

27   reality. Then, eleven months after the fact, she says her

28   husband's in Boston for the weekend when in reality he's

29   dead. And that's OK?

30 TODD: Yes.

31 JENNIFER: Todd, it isn't.

32 TODD: You'll get used to it.

33 JENNIFER: I don't want to get used to it. She should be forced

34   to — to —

35 TODD: To what? You pretend. You said so yourself. You color

1   your hair — which, incidentally, is a very becoming

2   shade. Come on.

3   JENNIFER: This situation is different, and you know it.

4   TODD: I don't think so.

5   JENNIFER: Honey, the whole situation is sick. Your mother

6   is sick, and you're —

7   TODD: And I'm sick for condoning it.

8   JENNIFER: I didn't say that. Oh, darling, let's not fight.

9   Please. You're defending a — a crazy woman. You know

10   it's wrong, but she's your mother so it's OK. But it isn't

11   OK. If she weren't your mother, you'd be saying the same

12   thing I am. And more. I know you.

13   TODD: My mother is not crazy.

14   JENNIFER: *(Wearily)* All right. She isn't. But she sure as heck

15   ain't sane.

16   TODD: *(Deliberately)* How marvelous to be you, my sweet. If it

17   isn't black, it's white. If it's not to your liking, we can't

18   have it.

19   JENNIFER: I'm not like that at all.

20   TODD: Oh? I'm glad to hear it.

21   JENNIFER: All right. Take any ten people you see and ask

22   them what they'd think of the situation. Go ahead.

23   TODD: I don't need to. I could ask a hundred people, and

24   they'd probably agree with you, but we're not talking

25   about a hundred people. We're talking about my mother

26   and my girl and me, and if they're a little different then

27   that's acceptable because they are who they are. And we

28   love them — for it, or despite it. Right?

29   JENNIFER: *(No answer.)*

30   TODD: Right, Jennifer?

31   JENNIFER: No, sweetheart. She's irrational. Her behavior

32   is irrational. *(TODD is silent. Stares.)* You say it's tolerable

33   because it's your mother. Well, all right. But as far as I'm

34   concerned, Todd, it isn't my mother, and it isn't all right.

35   It's creepy. It is. Deranged. Delusional. *(Giving way)* I

1	might as well say it, Todd. I hate it. I hate the way it
2	makes me feel. I wish I could get away from here. Now.
3	Not you, love. Here. This place.
4	TODD: You feel that strongly? My mother.
5	JENNIFER: It just isn't right.
6	TODD: All right, Jennifer. I respect your wishes. *(He goes to*
7	*the stairs and calls to MILLIE.)* **Mom?**
8	MILLIE: *(Off)* Honey?
9	TODD: I'll explain later, but I have to drive Jennifer to the
10	bus station now. She's leaving. I'll be back in about an
11	hour. OK? *(JENNIFER stares at him unbelieving.)*
12	MILLIE: *(Off)* Oh. Well. Certainly. Be careful, Todd. The
13	traffic seemed so heavy earlier.
14	TODD: I will. *(He and JENNIFER look at each other as we go to*
15	*black.)*
16	
17	
18	
19	
20	
21	
22	
23	
24	
25	
26	
27	
28	
29	
30	
31	
32	
33	
34	
35	

Behind the Scenes

RIDGELY HALLIDAY

27, a crisp, efficient, career-oriented woman; nice looking, dresses with a tailored look, good natured, has a guileless quality.

WIDEMAN DAVIS

A psychiatrist, 34, wears a mustache and beard, caustic sometimes, sure he knows all the answers.

SANDRA DONOVAN

An aging movie actress of 44 who admits to 31, a voice like dark velvet, husky, has "star quality", can be bitchy if she is out of sorts.

SCOTT NELSON

A handsome 25-year-old athlete who would rather play games than work; a so-so actor who gets by on his looks and charm.

1	*AT RISE:*	The living room of SANDRA DONOVAN's New England
2		home. Well furnished; many pictures of SANDRA. There is a
3		small entry hall leading to the outside and, of course, interior
4		doors. WIDEMAN DAVIS, SANDRA's psychiatrist, is reading.
5		Knocking can be heard at front door. He rouses himself to answer
6		it. RIDGELY HALLIDAY is off, comes in shortly.

7

8   **RIDGELY:**   **Oh, hello. I hope I'm at the right house.**

9   **WIDEMAN:**   **That all depends.**

10   **RIDGELY:**   **Sandra Donovan? Miss Donovan, the movie star?**

11   **WIDEMAN:**   **Yes?**

12   **RIDGELY:**   **Oh, thank heavens. I've been up and down this**
13   **road — I don't know how many times. Did you know**
14   **there's no street marker?**

15   **WIDEMAN:**   **We're well aware of it. It's one of the reasons Miss**
16   **Donovan lives here in the summertime.**

17   **RIDGELY:**   **I guess it is more private.**

18   **WIDEMAN:**   **And you have come for —**

19   **RIDGELY:**   **I am expected. I'm Ridgely Halliday. I'm —**

20   **WIDEMAN:**   **Ah, the writer. The ghostwriter.** *(Thinks he's clever.)*
21   **Shouldn't ghostwriters arrive in a white sheet?**

22   **RIDGELY:**   *(After a long pause, slightly annoyed)* **Was that supposed**
23   **to be funny?**

24   **WIDEMAN:**   **I'm sorry. It really was in bad taste, wasn't it?**
25   **Actually, I'm here as an employee of Miss Donovan's**
26   **myself. I'm Wideman Davis. Dr. Davis.**

27   **RIDGELY:**   **She's ill? Gosh, I just talked to her the other day.**
28   **Well, two weeks ago. How sick is she? I didn't realize —**

29   **WIDEMAN:**   **She's not, in the true sense of the word. Not sick**
30   **sick.** *(Slowly)* **You see, I'm not —** *(Sighs)* **you're going to be**
31   **here for a week or so, so you'll find out anyway. Sandra's**
32   **illness isn't physical.**

33   **RIDGELY:**   **You're her shrink?**

34   **WIDEMAN:**   **Her therapist, yes.**

35   **RIDGELY:**   **My roommate's seeing a shrink — a — a therapist.**

1	She's having sort of a — do they still call those things
2	where you don't feel good a nervous breakdown?
3	WIDEMAN: I believe you're talking about an anxiety reaction.
4	RIDGELY: I came at a bad time.
5	WIDEMAN: Well, I don't know. If she sent for you — she must
6	feel able to work. Have you ever seen her?
7	RIDGELY: Only on the screen. She looks gorgeous there. I
8	love her voice.
9	WIDEMAN: The "growl." Yes.
10	RIDGELY: It is a growl, isn't it? That's a good description.
11	Well — if I'm going to stay, I'd better get my luggage.
12	WIDEMAN: Need help? How many bags are there?
13	RIDGELY: I can manage. Honestly. Three.
14	WIDEMAN: There is a houseman of sorts. Actually, an
15	unemployed actor from New York who's pressing Sandra
16	to get him a role in her new picture.
17	RIDGELY: *(Starts off.)* Look, you don't have to help me.
18	WIDEMAN: *(Starts after her.)* Yes, I do. I'm guilt-ridden if I
19	don't offer.
20	RIDGELY: Oh, what a nutty thing to feel guilty about. And
21	you're a psychiatrist.
22	WIDEMAN: People are not consistent, Miss Halliday. *(They*
23	*both go off talking and reappear almost immediately with*
24	*RIDGELY's three bags.)*
25	RIDGELY: Ridder. Everyone calls me Ridder.
26	WIDEMAN: Call me "Weed" then.
27	RIDGELY: Thanks, Weed. I hate carrying stuff. But I'm
28	always doing it. If nothing else, it's my typewriter. *(Taps*
29	*the case she is carrying.)*
30	WIDEMAN: Ah, yes. And what do you do when you aren't
31	ghostwriting, ah — Ridder?
32	RIDGELY: Well, I write a daily column for the Columbus,
33	Ohio, newspaper. It's called "Tell it to Cora Sue."
34	WIDEMAN: And do they?
35	RIDGELY: The teen-agers do. In droves. How can they get

1 rid of their acne? How can they say no and still be friends
2 with someone? How about smoking?
3 WIDEMAN: And?
4 RIDGELY: Ask your doctor about the acne. Be honest with
5 yourself. And no, don't start.
6 WIDEMAN: That Cora Sue's a marvel.
7 RIDGELY: Well —
8 WIDEMAN: And now you're going to write some magnificent
9 prose for Sandra that will fall from those magnificent
10 lips at the Cannes Film Festival in April. She'll do you
11 proud, Ridder. She reads lines like a dream. Never had
12 an original thought in her head. They say she couldn't
13 ad-lib "pass the sugar," but once she gets her lines down,
14 that liquid voice takes over, and you'd swear you're in
15 the presence of one of the world's great brains.
16 RIDGELY: How do you know her so well, Weed? Do you — I
17 mean, you're not one of her ex-husbands?
18 WIDEMAN: No. Normally, we see each other about twice a
19 week, but she really has a problem this time.
20 RIDGELY: The actor who's pestering her to get him a job?
21 WIDEMAN: I don't think so. No. He just has to remember not
22 to give her the idea that he's using her friendship. That
23 makes her angry. And when Sandra gets angry —
24 SANDRA: *(We hear SANDRA and SCOTT NELSON yelling at*
25 *each other Offstage.)* Scott, I asked you an hour ago to go
26 downtown and get me a bottle of wine to serve at dinner.
27 Couldn't you just this once —
28 SCOTT: *(Off)* Cool it, will you, Sandra? Your cook gave me a
29 list of groceries three miles long she wants me to pick
30 up. The Mercedes needs servicing, and the garden hose
31 sprung a leak. I can only do — *(SCOTT comes on.)*
32 SANDRA: *(Off)* Why don't you admit it, darling? You're one of
33 the world's laziest slobs.
34 SCOTT: *(On stage. Angry for a moment.)* Hey, wait a minute.
35 SANDRA: *(Coming on, making an entrance. This must not be*

1	*caricatured.)* **And the only reason you're up here sponging**
2	**off me is to hook onto a job in my next film, which**
3	**incidentally is being shot in England. And I know you**
4	**love to work in England.**
5	WIDEMAN: Sandra, Miss Halliday is here.
6	SANDRA: *(Extends both hands; takes RIDGELY's hands.)* **Well,**
7	**darling, you** *are* **here. You must forgive the racket, Miss**
8	**Halliday.**
9	RIDGELY: I'm glad for the offer to work, Miss Donovan.
10	SANDRA: Just so you write some inspired lines for me to say
11	in Cannes, darling. No second-rate blather, you
12	understand. The last one who worked for me had the
13	most awful time getting the real me on paper. It was
14	rewrite, rewrite, rewrite. If I could only tell you how
15	exhausted I was when we finished.
16	SCOTT: You have told us, Sandra, dear. Over and over and
17	over and over.
18	SANDRA: *(Annoyed)* Meaning what?
19	SCOTT: Come on, Sandy. Lighten up.
20	SANDRA: *(Very much the great actress.)* Do we know each other
21	well enough for you to call me Sandy? I don't seem to
22	remember.
23	SCOTT: Forget it. I'll get the wine. And the groceries.
24	SANDRA: Do that.
25	SCOTT: I'll need some money. You know you can't charge at
26	the whiskey store.
27	SANDRA: Scott, does it ever make you self-conscious to be
28	constantly asking women for money? *(SCOTT glares at her.*
29	*He stands there, shaking his head from side to side, furious.)*
30	Tell cook I said she should —
31	SCOTT: Sandra, one of these days you're going to go too far
32	with that rotten disposition of yours. And when you do —
33	*(SCOTT exits quickly.)*
34	SANDRA: All right, Weed. Go ahead and tell me my insecurity
35	is showing again.

1	WIDEMAN: Is that what you think?
2	SANDRA: Oh, Weed! If once — just once — you'd express an
3	opinion. No. You have to turn every question back to me.
4	You must pray nightly to Carl Rodgers. *(WIDEMAN does*
5	*not answer.)* Now, let me talk to you a bit, Miss Halliday.
6	Your agency told me you used to write a daily column
7	for a paper in Columbus.
8	RIDGELY: I still do. I was telling Dr. Davis. It isn't anything
9	great. A question and answer column. Although it really
10	is quite popular. "Tell it to Cora Sue" they call it.
11	SANDRA: Cora Sue! Deliver me!
12	RIDGELY: Young people feel comfortable with it.
13	SANDRA: You write a column under an assumed name. Then
14	you work as a ghostwriter. So whatever you do, nobody
15	knows who you are. Little Miss Nothing. Or is it Little
16	Miss Nobody?
17	RIDGELY: Ghostwriting is a perfectly respectable profession,
18	Miss Donovan. After all, a woman's been writing speeches
19	for our presidents for years. And getting a lot of credit
20	for it, too. Do you do all your own stunts in a movie?
21	SANDRA: No, but then we're not talking about me, are we?
22	RIDGELY: The most famous women columnists in the United
23	States write under pseudonyms. People don't think any
24	less of them.
25	SANDRA: What — or who — are you hiding from, darling?
26	RIDGELY: I'm not hiding.
27	SANDRA: Really?
28	RIDGELY: *(Getting angry)* Look, Miss Donovan, you called me
29	for this assignment. If you want to call it off — get
30	someone else — it's OK. I have other work. No hard
31	feelings.
32	SANDRA: I'll look at your work first. The important thing is
33	that you get my personality down to a tee, Miss Halliday.
34	You watch what I do and how I do it. What I say. How I
35	say it. Get the feel of my expressions, the way I say things

1   — do you understand? *(Telephone rings.)*

2   RIDGELY: I've been successful with the other people I've

3   worked for. I have a knack for doing what you suggest ...

4   *(Telephone rings again.)*

5   SANDRA: Can someone get that? Where is Scott? Cook won't

6   lift a finger if it isn't the kitchen phone. *(Telephone again.)*

7   Weed, would you mind?

8   RIDGELY: I'll pick it up, Miss Donovan, if you like?

9   SANDRA: Weed.

10 WIDEMAN: *(Reluctantly answers phone.)* Hello ... Yes ... Just

11   a minute, please. *(Hands telephone to SANDRA.)* She wants

12   you.

13 SANDRA: Who is it?

14 WIDEMAN: Sandra, I am not your secretary.

15 SANDRA: *(Takes telephone.)* Yes? ... What? ... What do you

16   mean? ... Is this a joke? I see ... Yes ... Yes ... *(She hangs*

17   *up. There is silence. SANDRA starts to smile wickedly. There*

18   *is a long silence. The other two persons remain fixed. Finally:)*

19   Miss Halliday — or whatever your name is — what do you

20   think you're pulling here?

21 RIDGELY: Are you talking to me?

22 WIDEMAN: Sandra, calm yourself. Remember, I told you. I

23   want you to stop before you —

24 SANDRA: I mean, who are you?

25 RIDGELY: What are you talking about? You know who I am

26   and why I'm here.

27 SANDRA: I don't think so.

28 RIDGELY: What do you mean you don't think so?

29 SANDRA: That's what I'd like to know. That was Ridgely

30   Halliday on the phone just now. Calling to say she was

31   delayed and couldn't get here until tomorrow.

32 RIDGELY: That's a lie!

33 SANDRA: Is it? Weed, call the police.

34 WIDEMAN: Sandra, I told you before, I am not your secretary.

35 SANDRA: *(Looks from one to the other. Picks up the telephone,*

1	*dials 911.)* **Operator? This is Sandra Donovan . . . Yes, Old**
2	**Forest Road. Could you get the police out here as quickly**
3	**as possible?** *(The three continue to stare at each other. Who is*
4	*guilty here? Blackout.)*
5	
6	
7	
8	
9	
10	
11	
12	
13	
14	
15	
16	
17	
18	
19	
20	
21	
22	
23	
24	
25	
26	
27	
28	
29	
30	
31	
32	
33	
34	
35	

A Generous Allowance

Cast of Characters

IRA CALLENBERGER

*A banker, about 35, pleasant, tactful;
interested in the bank's customers.*

STANLEY FRAZER

*About 50, eccentric but knows what he's about;
sure of himself.*

CARTER BANFORD

*About 18, has a hustler's air about him; he is
unpleasant, cocky, lazy and unreliable.*

1   *AT RISE:*   Interior of a banker's office, nicely furnished, easy chairs,
2   draperies.
3
4   STANLEY: Now, Ira, I know as a banker — and a conservative
5   one at that — you're going to tell me I'm crazy.
6   IRA: Stanley, I'm not going to tell you anything.
7   STANLEY: But thinking of a scheme like this in the first
8   place —
9   IRA: It's your money, isn't it?
10 STANLEY: Absolutely.
11 IRA: Then why can't you open a checking account for your
12   dog, Spitzy?
13 STANLEY: *(Looks around nervously.)* Not so loud. I don't want
14   people to think I'm completely nuts. Nobody much minds
15   if you're a little funny, but if you push it too far —
16 IRA: Would that really worry you, Stanley?
17 STANLEY: Well — they already think I'm half-baked. That
18   outside stairway on my home that leads nowhere —
19 IRA: Now that you mention that, Stan, I've been wondering
20   about that myself.
21 STANLEY: Actually, it's not all that interesting. The contractor
22   went ahead and built it, then the architect said no, that
23   wasn't in the plans, then Herb said like hell it wasn't,
24   and now they're suing each other.
25 IRA: And you're stuck with the stairway.
26 STANLEY: I don't even see it anymore. But when word gets
27   around Spitzy has his own checking account at your
28   bank —
29 IRA: Stan, these things are confidential.
30 STANLEY: 'Till some employee finds it too good to keep.
31   Frankly, if I wasn't the one doing it, I'd think it was a
32   little off the wall myself.
33 IRA: Stan, we have wills leaving money to animals if the
34   owner dies or becomes incapacitated. Which reminds
35   me —

1	STANLEY: The point is, Ira, it isn't all a whim. Spitzy
2	actually has expenses.
3	IRA: OK.
4	STANLEY: His food, the main item. Grooming, haircuts,
5	baths, collars, coats, raincoats, checkups at the vet's —
6	immunization shots; room and board if he needed
7	hospitalization — if I'd ever get laid up, he'd need a
8	walker. If I couldn't get my nephew, Carter, to do it.
9	IRA: Speaking of Carter, how is he? I haven't seen him in
10	months.
11	STANLEY: Count your blessings. Carter is one of the world's
12	great con men, Ira. Rather than do a half-hour's work,
13	Carter, at age eighteen, would prefer spending three days
14	thinking how to get out of it. When people speak of no-
15	good bums and parasites in the world, the name that
16	should lead the list is my nephew, Carter Banford. But
17	he's my dear, dead sister's boy and one of my only two
18	living relatives.
19	IRA: So you give him money.
20	STANLEY: Not so much *give* as *put up*. I just put up
21	four-hundred dollars as a fine when they picked him up
22	for underage drinking. I'll also have to pay for his
23	counseling.
24	IRA: You think that's helping him?
25	STANLEY: No. I know it isn't. His therapist told me. I'm an
26	enabler. Enabling him to do it again. But how could I let
27	him sit in the can for two weeks? He's no good, but he's
28	only eighteen. He's my nephew and — *(He spreads his hands*
29	*in defeat.)*
30	IRA: You're making a mistake, Stan.
31	STANLEY: Well, look at it this way, Ira. In my own way, I'm
32	protecting myself too. The forty thousand I'm putting in
33	Spitzy's checking account is all the money I have. There's
34	the house and its contents and my two cars and other
35	possessions, but Spitzy's not about to sign a check for

1   Carter. So maybe that'll settle it with his asking me for
2   money in the future.
3 IRA: Come on, Stan. That's not you talking. You don't need
4   Spitzy as an excuse to turn him down. When you and I
5   were working on the United Way program, how did we
6   collect all that money?
7 STANLEY: Guts.
8 IRA: You've got it. Wait a minute, and I'll get a bank card for
9   Spitzy to sign — or stamp — or, well, what will he be
10   doing?
11 STANLEY: He'll be putting his paw down.
12 IRA: You may have to bring him in so we can witness his
13   signature — er — his paw.
14 STANLEY: Spitzy goes anywhere. *(IRA exits. STANLEY picks*
15   *up a magazine, leafs through it. A second later, CARTER appears*
16   *at the door.*
17 CARTER: *(Peeping in door)* Hey, Uncle Stan, baby. I thought
18   that was you.
19 STANLEY: Carter! What are you following me for?
20 CARTER: I wasn't.
21 STANLEY: Then how'd you know I was here?
22 CARTER: I didn't. I'm trying to hustle one of the tellers in
23   here — the little redhead — Jennifer — she told me she
24   saw you. And being the neighborly type, I thought I'd say
25   hello.
26 STANLEY: Well, Carter, that's very neighborly of you indeed.
27   But if you're thinking of asking me for money, or making an
28   investment or bailing you out of something, the answer
29   is go blow. Clear?
30 CARTER: Hey, that's not the friendly Uncle Stanley I know.
31 STANLEY: Yes, it is. I'll see you. Bye.
32 CARTER: Why do you always think I want something?
33 STANLEY: Past experience.
34 CARTER: OK, if that's the way it's going to go, how about
35   lending me two-hundred dollars?

1   STANLEY: For what?

2   CARTER: *(Fresh)* Did I ask you what you had for
3   breakfast?

4   STANELY: Carter, do me a favor. Hitchhike to California.

5   CARTER: You think more of your dog than you do of me.

6   STANLEY: He never let me down.

7   CARTER: You know what I believe? I believe you'd rather
8   give him the money than give it to me.

9   STANLEY: You're dead right.

10 CARTER: OK, joke around about it, Uncle. But one of these
11   days maybe you won't think it's so funny. You know,
12   Mom always said half of Grandpa's house that you're
13   living in belonged to her. But you never paid her a cent
14   for it.

15 STANLEY: Is that right?

16 CARTER: Yes. You gypped her out of it. So I'm only asking
17   for half of it since she never got it. That's only fair, isn't it?

18 STANLEY: Carter, *fair* isn't in your vocabulary. Unless
19   you're talking about a state fair.

20 CARTER: Once and for all, will you lend me the two hundred?

21 STANLEY: And once and for all, I told you my cash is all tied
22   up. Spitzy holds the purse strings. How often do I have
23   to say it?

24 CARTER: OK. You may regret your selfishness one day, Uncle
25   Stan. Just remember that. *(He starts to leave.)* You know,
26   I belong to an organization, Uncle. Not many people know
27   about it. And we're bound not to talk, but just remember,
28   when you're in a league with the great one — the Prince —

29 STANLEY: What kind of bunk are you putting through
30   yourself?

31 CARTER: The one and only, Uncle. The Prince of Darkness.

32 STANLEY: You're in a satanic cult? My God, Carter!

33 CARTER: Be careful, Uncle. There's ways to harm someone
34   without using physical force. And I'm telling you now —
35   some forces, once they're unleashed — can get out of

1   human control — can't be called back.

2   STANLEY: Carter, get out of here before I call the police.

3   CARTER: I'll do that, Uncle Stan. But just remember — *(Starts*

4   *to leave again. STANLEY breathes heavily, as if a chill had swept*

5   *over him. The two men stare at each other a second, then CARTER*

6   *swiftly leaves.)*

7   IRA: *(Re-enters.)* Here are the forms I was talking about, Stan.

8   *(STANLEY takes them.)* Wasn't that Carter I just saw?

9   STANLEY: One of your tellers told him I was here.

10   IRA: Someone has a big mouth.

11   STANLEY: It doesn't matter. Only — Ira, there's something I

12   want to discuss with you, and now's a good time —

13   IRA: What's wrong?

14   STANLEY: If anything should happen to me, I want you to take

15   care of Spitzy. Administer his — our — cash account. In

16   other words, act as the executor of my estate. I'll see my

17   lawyer about it today.

18   IRA: Stan, nothing's going to happen to you. You're only fifty.

19   You're healthy. You have enough money and investments to

20   live on. What are you talking about?

21   STANLEY: I'm talking about if anything *would* happen.

22   IRA: Stan, what's the matter?

23   STANLEY: I don't know. I do know Carter, however. And, Ira,

24   I'm not so much worried about myself as I am about Spitzy.

25   IRA: Spitzy?

26   STANLEY: Those — those satanic groups — they don't make

27   human sacrifices that I've ever heard about — but I have

28   read of them making — animal sacrifices.

29   IRA: Stan, you're letting your imagination run away with you.

30   STANLEY: I know. Carter may be eighteen to my fifty, and

31   maybe he thinks he has the dark prince in his corner, but

32   by darn, he'd better watch his step. I have a few tricks of

33   my own. And Nephew Carter would be foolish to forget

34   that — he really would — *(He remains very still gazing into infinity*

35   *as we go to black.)*

Out of the Tiger's Den

Cast of Characters

MARK CANFIELD
A retired lawyer of 65 who looks 45. Active, energetic, interested; a man of taste and some elegance.

CLAUDIA CANFIELD
Mark's wife, a little younger than he but the sort of woman who never grows old. Delightful, frank, a little guileless.

HARRY GUTHRIE
A factory worker, 35, frank, unexpectedly candid, likeable.

1   *AT RISE:*   The study of MARK and CLAUDIA CANFIELD is fairly
2   plush, reflecting taste and money. A card table has been set up
3   in the middle of the room with two chairs, some books and a
4   ream of paper. MARK is fiddling with papers at the table.
5   CLAUDIA is needlepointing. Silence pervades. Finally, there
6   is a knock on the door. CLAUDIA gets up first, then MARK.

7

8   CLAUDIA: Mark, before you open the door — I ought to go.
9   MARK: Why? You live here, too.
10   CLAUDIA: It might embarrass him. *(She starts to go.)* **You**
11   **know. Me sitting around.**
12   MARK: It's no big deal, Claudia. I'm going to try and teach a
13   thirty-five-year-old man to read and write. We don't need
14   to clear out the house.
15   CLAUDIA: I know. I just didn't want him to think I was one
16   of those wives who listen in.
17   MARK: You mean you're not going to?
18   CLAUDIA: Of course I'm going to. I'm as fascinated as you
19   are. But I don't want him to know that. *(Knocking comes*
20   *again.)* **You'd better open the door. He'll get discouraged.**
21   MARK: *(Throws open the door.)* **Harry? Harry Guthrie?**
22   HARRY: *(Off)* **Mr. Canfield?**
23   MARK: *(They shake hands.)* **Come in.**
24   HARRY: Am I late? The traffic was heavier than I figured.
25   MARK: Not at all. *(Turns to CLAUDIA.)* **This is my wife,**
26   **Claudia. Dear, this is Harry Guthrie.**
27   CLAUDIA: How do you do?
28   HARRY: OK.
29   MARK: *(They stand there awkwardly.)* **Well. Should we have a**
30   **try at it?**
31   HARRY: Huh?
32   MARK: Get started.
33   HARRY: Oh. Well — I thought — a friend of mine — Slime
34   Leightner — well, his real name's Clarence — he can't
35   read either. He goes to some guy up the line. Their first

1	night they just — you know — exchanged stories — what
2	they did for a living and stuff.
3	MARK: *(Snaps fingers.)* **An orientation night. Absolutely. I**
4	**should have thought of it myself.**
5	HARRY: **There's no rule, understand. It's not like you're**
6	**looking me over to — as if I wanted to marry your**
7	**daughter or anything.** *(He laughs uneasily.)*
8	CLAUDIA: **Our daughter is married.** *(All laugh.)* **Well, are you**
9	**a family man, Harry? Married? Divorced?**
10	HARRY: **Well — ah — no.**
11	MARK: **No what?**
12	HARRY: **No, not exactly married or divorced. But — me and**
13	**this woman are — seeing each other.**
14	MARK: **In my day, they called that dating.**
15	HARRY: **That's what she calls it. Only right now I work at a**
16	**plastics plant and they're loaded with orders, so what**
17	**with overtime, I can't —**
18	MARK: **What is your job?**
19	HARRY: **Shipping room clerk at B and J Plastics. Children's**
20	**stuff. Sand pails. Lunch buckets. Like that. That's why I**
21	**decided on doin' this. The way I am — they'd never give**
22	**a guy who can't read — I got no chance at advancement.**
23	**To get to be a big shot in the company — you have to do**
24	**more than just read orders. You gotta read everything.**
25	**Like say I get to be a buyer and I go in a restaurant with**
26	**one of our suppliers. How many times can I say, "You**
27	**read the menu, I forgot my glasses?"**
28	MARK: **You wear glasses?**
29	HARRY: **No.**
30	MARK: *(Laughs)* **Harry, I think you're pretty shrewd. You**
31	**have the best motivation I've ever heard.**
32	HARRY: **You can call me "Beans."**
33	MARK: **Beans?**
34	HARRY: **It's a nickname. They called my old man Beans. How**
35	**about you?**

1   MARK: Well — I was a lawyer. I *am* a lawyer. Retired.

2   HARRY: Yeah? Say, if you don't mind my asking, what would

3   a guy like you make an hour?

4   MARK: Well —

5   HARRY: I had to get a lawyer once. He did some work for me

6   on the old man's house when he died. I don't know if he

7   gypped me or not. What's your hourly rate?

8   MARK: You understand all a lawyer has to sell is his time?

9   HARRY: Me, too.

10   MARK: My fee was two-hundred dollars an hour when I

11   retired.

12   HARRY: *(Whistles. He is impressed.)* You gave that up to —

13   teach? They're not even paying you for this.

14   MARK: No. Because I believe in the organization that's

15   sponsoring this work. The Lawyers' Literary League of

16   Pennsylvania.

17   HARRY: You shoulda' held out for a salary, Mark. You're

18   going to deal with a twenty-four-carat dummy when you

19   take me on.

20   MARK: Well, I'll tell you — Beans, if it's going to be that

21   difficult, we'd better get started at that. *(Points to chair.)*

22   You sit over there if you will. I'll sit here. And I'll tell you

23   what we're going to do first.

24   CLAUDIA: Harry? Beans? *(HARRY turns to her.)* Do you mind

25   if I ask you something? I'm not part of the course, but —

26   HARRY: Shoot.

27   CLAUDIA: You're what? Thirty-five? And you just decided

28   you wanted to know how to read and write?

29   HARRY: Yeah.

30   CLAUDIA: After all these years?

31   HARRY: I didn't just decide it. It decided me. I got fed up

32   being the dummy.

33   CLAUDIA: You're far from a dummy.

34   HARRY: I'm not so sure. I know my A, B, C's. *(Starts to recite.)*

35   A, B, C, D, E, F ... *(His voice fades out as we go to black.)*

1	*(It is eight months later. Same den. The scene is empty. There*
2	*is a rap on the door, then the doorbell. Then another rap. Finally,*
3	*MARK comes in buttoning his shirt.)*
4	**MARK:** All right. All right. **I'm coming.** *(Throws open the door.*
5	*There is HARRY. Surprised.)* **Oh, it's you.**
6	**HARRY:** OK to come in?
7	**MARK:** *(Extends right arm as if to usher him in.)* **Enter and sign in.**
8	**HARRY:** I guess you're pretty teed-off at me.
9	**MARK:** Yeah, I'd say that.
10	**HARRY:** Understand, I don't blame you.
11	**MARK:** Harry, you and I had been working together for over
12	eight months until two-and-a-half weeks ago. Then you
13	disappeared. Swallowed up in the night. We were
14	supposed to meet twice a week, so that's five lessons
15	you've missed. Five nights I sat here — like some dummy,
16	as you so graphically put it, twiddling my thumbs waiting
17	for you to show up — which you didn't. And not only that,
18	you didn't even have the courtesy or the common decency
19	to call and explain you weren't coming. The question isn't
20	am I teed-off, Mr. Beans Guthrie. That isn't the question.
21	Of course I'm teed-off. The question is, who the hell do
22	you think you are?
23	**HARRY:** Look, you're one-hundred percent right. OK?
24	**MARK:** No, it isn't OK. Claudia was sure you were dead. I
25	called the league. They didn't know where you were. I
26	was going to call Slime Leightner, but the phone book
27	didn't list a Slime and I'd forgotten his real name.
28	**HARRY:** Clarence.
29	**MARK:** I see.
30	**HARRY:** I've been working a double shift. Six to two. Two to
31	ten. I couldn't make it out here at ten o'clock at night.
32	**MARK:** All right, even if you are telling the truth —
33	**HARRY:** I am telling the truth, Mark. What you're sore about
34	is that I didn't call.
35	**MARK:** You're damned right I am.

1   HARRY: I should have. That's a fault of mine. Never call
2   anybody. Even my girl friend calls me. Mark, you've been
3   a terrific guy to me. Don't think I don't appreciate it.
4   MARK: It's OK. I lost interest anyway.
5   HARRY: No!
6   MARK: Cool it, Beans.
7   HARRY: Cool it yourself. Mark, listen. I'm thirty-six. I've
8   been driving a car since I was sixteen. That's what?
9   Twenty years. All that time I never owned a car that
10   somebody else hadn't driven the guts out of first. It got
11   to be like a — a —
12   MARK: An obsession?
13   HARRY: Yeah. I make double time on overtime. Just once —
14   just once I wanted to own — I wanted to show my girl — I
15   wanted to see her expression when I tooled up in that
16   new car.
17   MARK: Harry, what you can't afford is not to finish.
18   HARRY: It worried me.
19   MARK: Besides, there's a reading contest in three weeks.
20   HARRY: What do you mean?
21   MARK: The league's sponsoring it. They give you something
22   to read you've never seen before. Fifteen people are in
23   it. But you could win.
24   HARRY: Me?
25   MARK: Yes. What's more, you're going to. I don't give a damn
26   if your girl friend throws you over or you drive a clunker.
27   I have eight months of my time invested in you. Eight
28   months of worrying and sweating and pushing you —
29   and — you've been great. Made me proud. And if you
30   think you're going to quit now and let me think I've made
31   a fool of myself, you've got another think coming.
32   HARRY: I couldn't win a reading contest if I stood on my
33   hands.
34   MARK: *(In command)* **Sit down, Beans.** *(He does.)* **Open your**
35   **book.** *(He does.)* **Now, begin. You are going to win. We're both**

1   going to win.

2   **HARRY:** *(Reads as we go to black.)* **"The sunset we saw from the**

3   **mountain was . . ."**

4   *(The den three weeks later. CLAUDIA, MARK and HARRY are*

5   *sitting around. No one seems very happy.)*

6   **HARRY:** Well, I warned you.

7   **MARK:** You did all right. You did better than all right. You

8   were the last to read. I heard the others. I tell you, you

9   weren't that bad.

10   **HARRY:** Who's kidding who? I tripped all over the place. Of

11   course, that crap — that junk they gave us to read —

12   **CLAUDIA:** Mark, how could they have picked a translation?

13   From French to English. *(Groans)* It wasn't even a good

14   translation.

15   **MARK:** What time is it? They said they'd call when they

16   reached a decision.

17   **CLAUDIA:** And that's another thing. What's the hocus-pocus

18   about they'd call? They could have decided then and

19   there. No, that'd make too much sense.

20   **HARRY:** I was a little nervous. That didn't help.

21   **MARK:** I tell you who wasn't bad. Your friend, Slime —

22   **HARRY:** Slime's no dummy.

23   **CLAUDIA:** Couldn't you get him a better name, Beans?

24   **HARRY:** He likes it. He refers to himself as Slime. Hey, look,

25   I'm keeping you folks up. Win or lose, I'm pooped. I'll give

26   you a call in the — *(Telephone rings. All three look at each*

27   *other, rooted to the spot. It rings again.)*

28   **CLAUDIA:** Well, answer it.

29   **MARK:** You.

30   **CLAUDIA:** It's for you. Nobody I know calls at this hour. It's

31   after eleven. *(Another ring)* Will you stop being silly and

32   answer it?

33   **MARK:** We lost. I can tell a losing ring when I hear it. Training

34   from my law days. *(Telephone rings again.)*

35   **CLAUDIA:** Oh, for heaven's sake. *(She goes to telephone.)*

1   **MARK:** I'll get it. *(Picks up telephone.)* **Mark Canfield — oh —**
2   **yes.** *(He starts to smile.)* **He didn't! He did. Oh, of course, I**
3   **didn't — here, talk to the man himself.** *(Hands phone to*
4   *HARRY who shakes his head no. He doesn't want to answer.)*
5   **Come on. It's the league president. Talk to him.**
6   **HARRY:** *(Takes phone.)* **Hello . . . This is Harry Guthrie . . .**
7   **Hey, how about that!** *(HARRY's conversation fades in the*
8   *background and what we really hear are CLAUDIA and MARK.*
9   *She takes his hand.)*
10   **CLAUDIA:** **Well, my dear. Very gratifying.**
11   **MARK:** **Well, I — I didn't do all that much.**
12   **CLAUDIA:** **You did and now you're loving every minute of it.**
13   **Admit it.**
14   **MARK:** **Of course I am. But even if he had lost, Claudia — the**
15   **fact that I was of help to him —**
16   **CLAUDIA:** **Help! You opened up a new world for him. I**
17   **wonder if he'll ever realize what you did. When he's**
18   **reading a newspaper or a book or a brochure at work,**
19   **or filling out a job application, or reading a menu, will**
20   **he stop and think that you — you did all that for him.**
21   **That you opened up his life — no — made his life.**
22   **Realized it for him.**
23   **MARK:** **It doesn't matter. Honestly. It really doesn't. What**
24   **does, I guess, is I was able to pay some of it back — the**
25   **education I was given.**
26   **CLAUDIA:** **Oh, Mark, you really are a dear.**
27   **MARK.** **Am I?**
28   **CLAUDIA:** **Yes. You are.**
29   **MARK:** *(Smiling)* **You're prejudiced. But I don't care. It's still**
30   **nice to hear. Now, I want to hear what he plans to do**
31   **from this point on.** *(He calls.)* **Hey, Beans!** *(Blackout)*
32
33
34
35

A Matter of Values

Cast of Characters

ALLEN MARKHAM

*20, handsome, athletic build, factory worker.
Bright, thoroughly nice, realistic.*

DAD MARKHAM

*60, with a slight limp. Good-looking, a
dreamer, immature at times.*

BABE HALLIWELL

*22, good-looking. Exhibits a "presence."
Strong-minded, sure of herself. Charmingly
forward.*

1   *AT RISE:*   The kitchen of the Markham house. DAD MARKHAM

2   is at the stove frying hamburgers. His wife is dead. A door slams

3   off camera and DAD picks up his head to listen.

4

5   DAD: *(Calls)* **Allen? Allen, is that you?**

6   ALLEN: *(Off)* **Dad?**

7   DAD: **In the kitchen, son. Come out and see if this is fit for**

8   **human consumption.**

9   ALLEN: *(Laughs coming on.)* **Hey, big daddy, you're a great**

10   **cook. Oops! Not hamburgers again.**

11   DAD: **I'm sick of them too, but they had a bargain on ground**

12   **beef at the Acme.**

13   ALLEN: **Who cares? I'll eat anything you put in front of me.**

14   *(Pause)* **Hey, what's wrong, Pop?**

15   DAD: **Nothing, really. Just thinking.**

16   ALLEN: **I was just kidding. I love hamburgers. It's un-American**

17   **not to like hamburgers.**

18   DAD: **It's not the hamburgers. I could put up with cheapie**

19   **meals — if there were anything else —**

20   ALLEN: **Dad, you've got a lot going for you.**

21   DAD: **I hear you. Shot up in Korea — a gimpy leg. Furloughed**

22   **from my job at the textile mill. Reduced to making meals**

23   **and keeping house for my twenty-year-old son.**

24   ALLEN: **I never had it so good.**

25   DAD: **Look at that piece in the paper, Allen.** *(Indicates*

26   *newspaper lying on chair.)*

27   ALLEN: *(Picks up newspaper.)* **Where?**

28   DAD: **On the second page.**

29   ALLEN: **Not this silly formal reception for Congressman**

30   **Eldridge?**

31   DAD: **It isn't silly. It would be a terrific plum to be invited.**

32   **But we're nobodies.**

33   ALLEN: **You can't get over being the football hero of the**

34   **forties, can you?**

35   DAD: **I was more than that. I was the best looking guy in the**

1   senior class. The most popular fellow in town.

2 ALLEN: And the most modest!

3 DAD: They voted me that in the yearbook. But when you
4   marry young and poor, you may not stay young, but you
5   certainly stay poor. The richest girl in Bentonville had
6   the "hots" for me.

7 ALLEN: I believe it.

8 DAD: Sylvia Duxberry. Wasn't bad looking either. Her daddy
9   had a chain of fifty grocery stores. But there was your
10   mother, Eleanor Dixon, the head cheerleader. *(Slow —*
11   *caught in nostalgia.)* We were so in love. And we thought
12   it would always be Saturday — after the game — and
13   we'd won . . . *(Pause)* If I only had it to do over.

14 ALLEN: You'd do the same thing.

15 DAD: Well, you're not going to make that mistake. My life's
16   over. But you — you're young — you're even better
17   looking than I was.

18 ALLEN: If that's possible.

19 DAD: It isn't just being invited to Congressman Eldridge's
20   testimonial dinner that's important, Allen. What I always
21   dreamed of was for you to meet him, have him see what
22   a great guy you are — athlete and student — hell, you
23   were at the top of your class — then have him give you
24   an appointment to one of the service academies. West
25   Point. Annapolis. The Air Force Academy. That's where
26   the action is — where the contacts are made and kept in
27   later life. All those guys have sisters, too. This way you
28   can't afford any college, even with an athletic
29   scholarship. To borrow the money — that's not my way
30   of doing things, and I don't want it for you, either.

31 ALLEN: Dad, I have a decent job at the cabinet factory. It's
32   second shift, but I'm a foreman. I'm making good money.
33   I have a nice girl, Cindy Thomas.

34 DAD: Son, what you're talking about is — well, second-rate.
35   Not your Cindy. But the factory manager could lay you

1	off any time. Discharge you if you happen to say the
2	wrong thing to the wrong person. A professional man — a
3	career officer — they're positions that count. It's as easy
4	to fight for a better life as it is to give in to one that's
5	second-rate.
6	ALLEN: Poor old Pop.
7	DAD: Say, you have some personal days coming at work,
8	don't you?
9	ALLEN: At least ten.
10	DAD: Stay home tonight. Just the two of us. I'll make popcorn,
11	and we'll watch the fights on television.
12	ALLEN: Dad, I can't. Some VIP is coming through the plant
13	on my shift, and Mr. Flexner's already spoken to me about
14	showing whoever it is around.
15	DAD: No one ever won a trophy for not taking his personal
16	days when he wanted to.
17	ALLEN: Dad, you should get a job.
18	DAD: Get out of here!
19	ALLEN: Be a volunteer then. Foster grandfather at our local
20	instituion for the mentally retarded. Maybe bagging
21	groceries at the Acme.
22	DAD: Me? No, thanks. I'm a worn-out, old has-been, but if I
23	can't go and do the things I want to, I'll stay home. And
24	that's just what I'm doing.
25	ALLEN: Things are different now.
26	DAD: Not on your life. Money and connections may not bring
27	happiness into your life, but they sure as heck don't keep
28	it out either. If only I had remembered that! *(We go to*
29	*black.)*
30	*(ALLEN's office at the cabinet factory. He is on the telephone.)*
31	ALLEN: Third floor. Allen Markham speaking . . . Oh, yes,
32	Mr. Flexner. Oh, so that's who's here . . . Yes, I've seen
33	her on television . . . Babe Halliwell . . . Well, who
34	hasn't? . . . Yes, I understand . . . Absolutely . . . thank
35	you . . . *(Replaces telephone. Gives his hair a fast comb. A second*

1		*later, BABE HALLIWELL strides in with a camera around her neck.)*
2	BABE:	Mr. Markle?
3	ALLEN:	Markham. Allen Markham. And you're Miss Halliwell?
4	BABE:	*(Dynamic)* Here to do a piece on industry in America.
5	ALLEN:	Great.
6	BABE:	Do you realize Americans are beginning to use
7		nothing but products made overseas, Mr. Markle?
8	ALLEN:	Markham.
9	BABE:	Yes. The electronics industry, cars, computers, clothes
10		— if it isn't made in Taiwan, it's made in Hong Kong. Or
11		in Austria. Or Great Britain. Or West Germany.
12	ALLEN:	That's the old fight.
13	BABE:	Where do you think we ought to start, ah —
14	ALLEN:	Allen.
15	BABE:	"Handsome" would be better.
16	ALLEN:	Thank you, but the company has a rule — no
17		flattering the second shift foreman.
18	BABE:	Does it embarrass you to have a woman call you
19		handsome?
20	ALLEN:	Well, my dad calls me that too, but he's prejudiced.
21	BABE:	What are you doing? Working here between college
22		semesters?
23	ALLEN:	I'm not in school.
24	BABE:	You look like you should be in the scrimmage line of
25		one of the big ten.
26	ALLEN:	Quarterback. My old — my dad played the same
27		position when he was in high school.
28	BABE:	A home-town glamour boy.
29	ALLEN:	Not likely. What part of the plant were you interested
30		in seeing, Miss Halliwell?
31	BABE:	Call me Babe. And I think I'm seeing it.
32	ALLEN:	*(Amused as well as taken aback. Laughs in spite of*
33		*himself.)* Hey, you come on sort of —
34	BABE:	Fast and furious. How old you are, Allen?
35	ALLEN:	I'll be twenty-one next month.

1   BABE: I'm twenty-two, and I've learned —

2   ALLEN: You've come pretty far in a short time. Your own

3   special investigative report show on television, world

4   traveler —

5   BABE: I could never afford to be a shrinking violet — never

6   had time. I also learned men who are secure with

7   themselves don't mind a girl with a little spunk. If I bowl

8   them over, they were never for me in the first place.

9   ALLEN: You've got style, all right. And, no, you don't scare me.

10   BABE: Good, because I was wondering how you'd like to go

11   out for something to eat after you finish work. I'm a night

12   owl anyway.

13   ALLEN: Well, thanks, but — I usually go home.

14   BABE: Married?

15   ALLEN: *(Laughs)* No. Not even near it, although I've been

16   seeing someone weekends. No, my Dad waits up for me.

17   It's only him and me. We catch up on the local news at

18   eleven, then the national scene later.

19   BABE: Well, I'm going to be here a week or so. If you can't go

20   tonight, how about lunch tomorrow?

21   ALLEN: That sounds pretty good — on one condition.

22   BABE: *(As if warned)* Oh-oh.

23   ALLEN: That I pay.

24   BABE: I can't ask you out for lunch, then let you pay. We'll

25   go Dutch treat.

26   ALLEN: I pay.

27   BABE: You want to do this?

28   ALLEN: Who could turn down an invitation like that from a

29   woman as beautiful as you. *(Blackout.)*

30   *(The next day, after lunch. ALLEN and BABE are sitting in a*

31   *restaurant booth.)*

32   BABE: Oh, I'm stuffed. The food is delicious here. Do you

33   come often?

34   ALLEN: Pop cooks. Hamburgers. He's retired from the

35   service. Mom died nine years ago.

1 BABE: Would you believe I only get home at Christmas time?
2   It's been that way for years — even when I was attending
3   Radcliffe. Then I went right to work for Television News.
4 ALLEN: You really are a success story. But I can see why.
5 BABE: I don't suppose you'd be free to go to the Eldridge
6   testimonial dinner with me Friday night?
7 ALLEN: The — the Eldridge reception?
8 BABE: The congressman's a friend of my family. Dad called
9   and told him I was here. He got in touch with me at the
10   hotel the minute I arrived and insisted I come.
11 ALLEN: I see.
12 BABE: What do you say, Allen? The congressman'll fix me up
13   with a date if you won't go. You know what that'll be. All
14   teeth and no chin. Do you have a dinner jacket?
15 ALLEN: I can get one in twenty-four hours. A friend I went
16   to high school with has a store downtown.
17 BABE: Is it a date?
18 ALLEN: I — I — so Congressman Eldridge is really a personal
19   friend?
20 BABE: Not only that. He owes me a favor. I had him on my
21   show one night, and the old boy loved it. All that
22   attention. His own make-up man, his personal escort. He's
23   dying to come on again.
24 ALLEN: I'll pick you up about six. At your hotel.
25 BABE: Make it seven, and I'll pick you up. Now, don't fuss.
26   My company put a limo at my disposal, and the Eldridge
27   bash doesn't start until seven-thirty. You know, I have
28   an idea this is one reception I'm going to enjoy.
29 ALLEN: You took the words out of my mouth. Or my dad's . . .
30 *(And we go to black.)*
31
32
33
34
35

Finding the Right Key

Cast of Characters

STELLA ARNOLD

A charming, personable woman, 34. Wife, mother, untidy, disorganized and very loving.

RANDY ARNOLD

Her husband, age 35. Handsome, quick to argue, but really a caring person.

PAMELA ARNOLD

Age 12, their daughter. Bright, sensitive, fresh, verbal, daring and intuitive. If she weren't so darling, she'd be a brat.

JUNIOR ARNOLD

Age 10, average, perceptive, guileless. Being the younger brother to Pamela has not been easy for him.

1   *AT RISE:*   The Arnold kitchen is cozy, warm, large and cluttered.
2   There is too much of everything needed in a kitchen, and a lot
3   of what isn't. There is a table and four chairs where the family
4   dines. When the scene opens, STELLA ARNOLD is discovered
5   at the stove making breakfast. STELLA has an abstract sort of
6   charm — as if she were frying eggs, but in reality, listening to
7   a Mozart aria and perhaps singing along with it.
8
9   STELLA: *(Calling)* **Pamela! Junior! Breakfast!**
10   JUNIOR: *(Off)* **OK, Mom. I'm coming.** *(Running in)* **Oh, boy,**
11   **pancakes! Lemme at 'em!**
12   PAMELA: *(Off)* **Stella, I can't find Caesar.**
13   STELLA: **If you're referring to your Latin book, Pamela, it's**
14   **on the piano.**
15   PAMELA: *(Coming in. She has a marvelous self-assurance. She*
16   *also has a wild hairdo.)* **People are forever hiding things**
17   **around here. Good morning, Mom.**
18   STELLA: **Good morning, darling. What have you done to**
19   **your hair?**
20   JUNIOR: **She copied it out of a movie book. I seen her.**
21   PAMELA: **"Saw," Junior. You use the past tense with —**
22   JUNIOR: **OK, so you still don't look like a rock star. Hi ya,**
23   **Pop.**
24   RANDY: *(Descending scale. Comes in. He likes girls, and while in*
25   *love with STELLA, can be turned by flattery. At the moment he*
26   *is in excellent humor.)* **Good morning! Good morning! Good**
27   **morning! Stella, darling, did anyone ever tell you you're**
28   **very lovely in the morning?**
29   STELLA: **Morning, Randy. Thank you, darling. You're a**
30   **handsome gent yourself.**
31   RANDY: **But I'm very modest about it.**
32   STELLA: **Simply another of your charms.**
33   RANDY: **Boy — I feel good this morning. I'm so hungry, I**
34   **could eat a cow. Where's the paper?**
35   PAMELA: **Miss Symington says it's very rude to read at the**

1	table. Miss Symington says if you aren't interested in the
2	people you're eating with, you shouldn't eat with them.
3	Pass the jam, please.
4	RANDY: Really? And what does Miss Symington say about
5	twelve-year-olds who give free advice to their parents?
6	PAMELA: My being twelve is beside the point. Mentally, I'm
7	eighteen and a half.
8	RANDY: Well, Miss Eighteen and a Half, get on with your
9	breakfast. You too, Junior.
10	JUNIOR: Don't disturb me. I'm thinking.
11	STELLA: Well, stop it. All you think about is how to kill us.
12	And no more setting your booby traps in the bathroom,
13	do you hear?
14	RANDY: Let him alone, Stella. It's healthy for youngsters to
15	invent things.
16	PAMELA: Oh, Randy's right, Stella. You can't stifle his
17	creative impulses.
18	RANDY: And make her stop calling me "Randy." Is that all
19	she learns at the school for the gifted?
20	STELLA: Well, you wanted her to go there.
21	RANDY: Me! I wanted her to go there! Who found Miss
22	Symington in the first place?
23	PAMELA: There's no point arguing about it. I'd be stifled in
24	an ordinary school.
25	JUNIOR: If I had some explosive powder, I could fix a
26	humdinger.
27	PAMELA: "Humdinger." Isn't he quaint, Stella?
28	RANDY: No, he isn't quaint. He's normal. And stop calling
29	your mother Stella.
30	PAMELA: Miss Symington says — and I quote — "Equality of
31	all people is the keynote of democracy." End of quote.
32	RANDY: For heaven's sake, Stella, do something about her.
33	STELLA: Darling, she's your child, too.
34	PAMELA: You shouldn't discuss things like that in front of
35	me. Makes me feel I'm not wanted.

1	STELLA:	That's enough for one morning, Pamela. Eat your
2		breakfast.
3	RANDY:	*(Vicious sweetness; starting in low gear.)* **Stella — dear.**
4	STELLA:	What is it, Randy?
5	RANDY:	The coffee, dear.
6	STELLA:	Why, Randy, I thought that was exactly the way
7		you liked it.
8	RANDY:	Nobody could possibly be expected to like coffee
9		that looked like mud and tasted like hemp. Come on,
10		now — you forgot to use the measuring cup, didn't you?
11	STELLA:	Nonsense. I measured it exactly.
12	RANDY:	Lying is probably one of the least convincing of your
13		few genuine accomplishments. That coffee is awful!
14	JUNIOR:	Oh-oh. Hang on, sis. Here we go again.
15	STELLA:	And I wish you wouldn't shout at me in front of the
16		children. I'm sure it's bad for their — their what-do-you-
17		call-its.
18	RANDY:	I'm not shouting.
19	PAMELA:	That's silly. Of course you're shouting. But we
20		don't mind, Randy. We like it.
21	RANDY:	You keep out of this. Stella, what were you doing
22		when you weren't measuring out the coffee grounds?
23	STELLA:	I was merely trying to get my weekly article for the
24		Courier finished. After all, I couldn't get anything written
25		last night, could I?
26	RANDY:	Ye gods! If only just once you wouldn't use those
27		piffling little articles you write for the Courier as an
28		excuse for your utter inadequacy as a wife and
29		mother . . .!
30	STELLA:	They're not piddling!
31	RANDY:	They are — and besides, I said piffling.
32	JUNIOR:	Oh, boy, this looks like a good one!
33	RANDY:	Be quiet, you two! Go to school or something . . .
34	STELLA:	*(Going blithely on as if never interrupted.)* **And those**
35		piddling little articles, as you call them, have already

1   gotten me offers from two New York papers.

2   **RANDY:**   They're just trying to encourage you.

3   **STELLA:**   Just the same, one of those offers might come in

4   handy some day!

5   **RANDY:**   There you go — threatening to leave again . . . !

6   **STELLA:**   I never threaten. You wait and see.

7   **PAMELA:**   We don't think she means it either, Pop.

8   **STELLA:**   You just wait — you'll be sorry when I'm — *(Clean*

9   *break)* Oh, Randy, we're doing it again. Oh, darling, please,

10   let's stop.

11   **RANDY:**   *(Hotly)* Well, if that isn't just like a — *(Breaks, too.)*

12   You know, I don't even remember what got us started.

13   **STELLA:**   Something silly. It always is.

14   **PAMELA:**   Well, Pop said the coffee tasted like jute, and then

15   you brought up those Courier articles again, and —

16   **STELLA:**   Yes, Pamela. That will do. Now, both of you. Off to

17   school. Mother means it.

18   **PAMELA:**   Don't talk about yourself in the third person,

19   Stella. It sounds childish. Come on, Stinky. This one's

20   blown over. We might as well get going. *(Starts off.)* So

21   long, Randy . . .

22   **RANDY:**   So long, kids. See you later.

23   **JUNIOR:**   *(Going off)* Bye, Pop. Bye, Mom. *(We hear the door open*

24   *and slam closed.)*

25

26

27

28

29

30

31

32

33

34

35

A Joyous Holiday

Cast of Characters

STELLA TEDDIMAN

*65, intense, a beautiful woman now faded.
A homemaker, well dressed.*

CLAIRE TEDDIMAN

*Stella's daughter, age 39. Fragile, too tightly
strung, loving, suffers from migraine
headaches.*

Note

*This piece needs careful attention. STELLA,
the mother, loves CLAIRE almost fanatically.
She wants her to marry a man who is rich,
handsome, prominent, loving, kind — in
short, a man who doesn't exist. CLAIRE
knows this but doesn't want to hurt her mother
either. So she is caught between the real world
and the one her mother dreams of for her.
STELLA is played with a light foreign rhythm
to her speech.*

1 *AT RISE:*   The living room of the Teddiman apartment. The furniture
2   is nice but aging. CLAIRE comes wearily in. STELLA is on the
3   telephone. An oppressive air seems to pervade the place.
4
5 STELLA: *(On telephone)* ... Now, Emily, everybody knows
6   about her. Charge accounts all over town and doesn't
7   pay a soul. If I can't pay for it, I do without ... Well, here's
8   my little girl. My baby just walked in ... Tonight? *(She*
9   *laughs affectedly.)* Oh, busy, busy, busy. You know the
10   young girls nowadays. Never satisfied with one fellow. I
11   can't tell you how many nights she could go out if she
12   wanted. Claire, I'm going to move the telephone next to
13   your bed, I keep telling her. If I get one call a week, I'm
14   lucky ... Yes ... Well, Happy New Year to you ... Bye.
15   *(Replaces receiver. Exhales noisily.)* Whew ... that woman
16   talks your ear off when she gets started. It's a physical
17   effort to talk to her.
18   *(During speech, STELLA's voice is heard, but camera is on*
19   *CLAIRE as she first gets aspirin bottle from shelf in kitchen,*
20   *shakes several tablets from it, then gets a glass, fills it with water.*
21   *She stands wearily by the sink when STELLA enters.)*
22 STELLA: *(Cont.)* **What's the matter? Your head again?** *(CLAIRE*
23   *nods grimly, takes tablets.)* **Why don't you listen to me and**
24   **see a doctor, honey? Claire?**
25 CLAIRE: I talked to Dr. Bradigan. They can't do anything for
26   migraines.
27 STELLA: How do you know? Brad isn't the last doctor in the
28   world.
29 CLAIRE: I'll lie down for a while, Mother. I'll feel better then.
30 STELLA: After supper. We're having steak. Steak is only
31   good made and eaten.
32 CLAIRE: I'm not hungry.
33 STELLA: Honey, I made baked potatoes, a chef salad —
34 CLAIRE: Maybe — later.
35 STELLA: Later, I want to get dressed. So do you.

1   CLAIRE: No, I'm not going anywhere — special.
2   STELLA: You're not — you mean Sid didn't — *(Suddenly)*
3   You're not giving him that sweater you bought for his
4   birthday next week?
5   CLAIRE: *(Smiles)* **No.**
6   STELLA: The minute I saw him, I could read that Sidney
7   Conley like a book.
8   CLAIRE: Mother, I don't want to discuss it.
9   STELLA: Forgive me. The subject's closed. We still have to
10   eat. Honey, it makes it so late with the dishes otherwise.
11 CLAIRE: *(Decides to take the plunge.)* **Mother —** *(STELLA looks*
12   *up.)* **Miss Beilor** — she's my field supervisor —responsible
13   for six counties — she was in the office this morning. They
14   need a county supervisor in a little town near Erie.
15   Around the middle of March.
16 STELLA: *(Disregarding CLAIRE's news momentarily)* **From the**
17   very first night, I suspected that Sidney was an eighteen-
18   carat tightwad.
19 CLAIRE: What I wanted to say is — Miss Beilor hinted
20   around to see if I would be interested in the job. It would
21   be a nice promotion. When you work for the state welfare
22   office, they say you shouldn't turn down a promotion.
23 STELLA: *(Not really listening.)* **What promotion?**
24 CLAIRE: That town near Erie. Supervisor. Around the
25   middle of March.
26 STELLA: Erie? I was there once with your father. As a town,
27   it's a dead issue.
28 CLAIRE: Of course, we only talked. But I thought it might be
29   a change for the two of us.
30 STELLA: So that's it. Now we're leaving Kingston. Where we
31   were born and raised.
32 CLAIRE: Don't get mad, Mom. I only mentioned it. Nothing
33   definite.
34 STELLA: I work and slave for my children. All my life, my
35   children came first.

1	CLAIRE:	I know.
2	STELLA:	The livelong day I'm stuck in this house. I don't go
3		anywhere. I don't see anyone.
4	CLAIRE:	Mom, look — I didn't mean anything. Please —
5	STELLA:	It kills me to see you going to that office at eight-
6		thirty in the morning, day after day. What kind of a life
7		is that for a girl? I tried to raise my children nicely.
8	CLAIRE:	*(She's heard it all so often.)* Oh, heavens.
9	STELLA:	You show me another girl in this town who —
10	CLAIRE:	Please, Mom — let's drop it.
11	STELLA:	Now I'm not even allowed to talk. All day long I
12		have nobody to talk to —
13	CLAIRE:	*(Lifts her voice.)* Mom, I'm tired.
14	STELLA:	My whole life starts when you come home. Don't
15		set your glass on that table. I just finished cleaning in
16		here.
17	CLAIRE:	Then let me sit in peace a minute.
18	STELLA:	You wanted to go to California five years ago. All
19		right, go on, go. You stayed a year. Nothing. Philadelphia
20		three years ago. Another failure. Every summer you
21		spend three weeks at your brother Ed's in Syracuse. What
22		more can I give you?
23	CLAIRE:	I'm not blaming you.
24	STELLA:	I made two meals for that Sidney that were
25		knockouts. Weren't they knockouts? To please you.
26	CLAIRE:	I know. And I —
27	STELLA:	What do you want from me?
28	CLAIRE:	Nothing. I don't know. I thought maybe for a change
29		— I'd meet someone. You never liked —
30	STELLA:	I never liked! I never liked! That insurance man
31		from Harristown ten years ago. That man didn't make a
32		living, didn't finish high school. He didn't even have a
33		decent suit on his back. Do you want him?
34	CLAIRE:	I don't know — now.
35	STELLA:	When Daddy was sick, I needed you. There was

time then. The last fellow you brought here — Ted
Christie — a divorced man with three children. The wife
an alcoholic. Was that a situation to get into?

CLAIRE: No, I suppose not. But, Mom, I'm thirty-nine years
old.

STELLA: The prime of life. I gave everything —

CLAIRE: You've told me.

STELLA: Everything so you could be married. But to the
right man.

CLAIRE: Now — I can't stop hoping. I can't stop! *(She puts
her hand over her mouth.)* **Oh.** *(She breaks into tears. STELLA
stands in bewilderment. Blackout.)*

A Short Trip

Cast of Characters

ANNE WETHERILL

24, nice, pretty, rich, spoiled, sensible. Likes her own way, impulsive, in love with Jack.

TRISH WETHERILL

28, her sister. A snob, impressed with her money, complains continually, doesn't work. Yet there are traces of decency, too. Remember: no character is all good or all bad. Look for shadings of grey.

JACK BRAMLEY

29, a nice guy. A little rough around the edges, loves Anne if he can come to grips with her money. A non-commissioned officer in the U.S. Navy stationed at San Diego, California.

1 *AT RISE:* The restaurant at a railroad station near San Diego.
2   JACK and ANNE are sitting in a booth with a big picture
3   window. Beyond are moving trains. The couple is having coffee
4   waiting for ANNE's sister, TRISH (Patricia) to arrive. JACK
5   isn't thrilled at the prospect of the visit. ANNE is thrilled.
6
7 JACK: **Stop jumping up and down, Sugar. It's only your**
8   **sister we're meeting.**
9 ANNE: **But Jack, it's been six months since we've seen each**
10   **other. It's darned nice of her to come out to California**
11   **just to see me.**
12 JACK: **Yeah, San Diego in January. What a tough break for**
13   **Trish. I'm still surprised she insisted on coming by train.**
14 ANNE: **She won't fly. Not since Mom died in that plane crash.**
15 JACK: **But honey, that was five years ago. And in India to boot.**
16 ANNE: **It's the way she feels. That's why we're meeting the**
17   **train.**
18 JACK: **How long is she going to stay?**
19 ANNE: **A couple of months, if I can talk her into it. I hate my**
20   **apartment when you're not around. Just me rattling**
21   **about in seven rooms.**
22 JACK: **Which your salary at the Red Cross doesn't begin to**
23   **cover.**
24 ANNE: **You love to remind me of that, don't you?**
25 JACK: **It's the truth.**
26 ANNE: **Daddy's monthly check comes in handy. I'll admit**
27   **that. But I am working —**
28 JACK: **For a change.**
29 ANNE: *(Mock outrage)* **Jack!**
30 JACK: **Just a little joke.**
31 ANNE: **More important, I'm in San Diego where you're**
32   **stationed.**
33 JACK: *(Gratefully)* **And that's the greatest part, Anne.**
34 ANNE: **If only you weren't so stubborn.**
35 JACK: **Anne, I'm on the verge of being shipped to the Middle**

1   East. Those countries are in the middle of an undeclared
2   war. After I get back and I'm assigned somewhere, then
3   we'll talk marriage. OK?
4 ANNE: No.
5 JACK: Come on. You agreed.
6 ANNE: I change my mind on occasion. *(JACK looks surprised.)*
7   Don't look so shocked. You knew that. *(Sees her sister*
8   *through window.)* Oh, Jack. There she is!
9 JACK: *(Looks)* Where?
10 ANNE: There. Over there coming out on the platform. Behind
11   all those suitcases. In that chinchilla jacket.
12 JACK: Look, you wait here. I'll get her.
13 ANNE: No, you wait. *(She restrains him with a hand movement.)*
14   Please, honey. It'll work best this way.
15 JACK: Look, we'll both go. *(They exit swiftly. Blackout.)*
16   *(A train station platform. TRISH is standing in the middle of*
17   *ten or twelve suitcases. Her arms are crossed over each other and*
18   *she is drumming her fingers impatiently. She is very chic, very*
19   *well dressed.)*
20 ANNE: *(Coming on, followed by JACK.)* Trish! Trish, darling.
21   Here we are. *(Waves hands. The two women rush to embrace.)*
22 TRISH: Anne, darling.
23 ANNE: Oh, I'm so glad to see you.
24 JACK: *(Finally)* 'Lo, Patricia. *(He and TRISH press cheeks.)*
25 TRISH: Hello, Jack.
26 ANNE: *(Draws back to inspect TRISH who twirls to show off.)* And
27   a new chinchilla jacket. I'm burning with envy.
28 TRISH: *(Preening)* Oh, like it, Anne? I wasn't going to —
29   *(Sincerely)* All those homeless people on the streets — that
30   gets to you — even someone as selfish as I am — *(Back to*
31   *spoiled, rich girl)* Then I thought — well, the furriers have
32   to live too.
33 ANNE: How was the trip?
34 TRISH: Don't ask. Don't say a word. Every bone in my body
35   aches. And I have listened to the beautiful but sad stories

1	of at least six mill girls. Why do you suppose they pick
2	me to confide in?
3	ANNE: Because you encourage it. You ask questions.
4	TRISH: Oh, I don't. I don't do that, do I?
5	JACK: Say, are all those bags yours?
6	TRISH: There should be ten. Or is it twelve? I have it written
7	down somewhere. Darling, where are the redcaps around
8	here?
9	JACK: *(Patiently)* Trish, there are no redcaps anymore.
10	They're all in better paying jobs. No one wants to do work
11	like that anymore. Why do you suppose every store and
12	restaurant in the United States is advertising for help?
13	TRISH: *(She only hears what she wants to.)* But, Jack, you can't
14	manage all those by yourself. Or can you?
15	ANNE: Look, I can carry three. Jack can take four. You take
16	those three little ones, Trish.
17	TRISH: But, Anne, I only have two hands. You know my back.
18	JACK: *(Very patiently)* It's only through the station.
19	ANNE: I rented a van.
20	JACK: Wait. Wait a minute. I'll get one of those station carts.
21	I saw one parked somewhere when we came in. *(He rushes
22	off and returns in a moment with a cart.)*
23	TRISH: Honestly, this is just typical of the whole trip. It's
24	worth your life to travel, Anne. Every time I went to the
25	train diner, it was wall-to-wall people. Then one night
26	they seated these three terrible looking characters at my
27	table. Seated them if you please, *then* asked me if it'd be
28	all right. I mean, really!
29	ANNE: *(Helping load cart)* Oh, what are you carrying around?
30	Bricks?
31	TRISH: That must be the one with the shoes. Let Jack handle
32	that.
33	JACK: *(Loading)* I don't have anything between my teeth.
34	TRISH: Is he serious?
35	ANNE: Trish, maybe you did go overboard.

1   TRISH: Anne, you know me. I can't go anywhere if I'm not
2   dressed right.
3   JACK: *(Caustically)* **If only you could have recruited one of**
4   **those awful-looking people in the diner to help you.**
5   ANNE: Jack! You promised.
6   TRISH: Oh, he's right. Those men all had muscles with tattoos
7   — oh, that isn't the way you meant it at all.
8   ANNE: Let's get going. We can talk back at the apartment.
9   JACK: I'm not coming back.
10   ANNE: *(Upset)* Jack. Don't say that.
11   JACK: You two will want to talk. I'll only be in the way.
12   TRISH: Anne, if he feels like that, maybe — it would be
13   simpler.
14   ANNE: At least ride with us, and I can drop you off.
15   TRISH: Then we'll all be squashed in the car together. I hate
16   that. You know my claustrophobia. Really, Anne, you
17   might have managed a little better.
18   JACK: Look, sister, are you going to stop that complaining?
19   TRISH: Well, really — and whom do you think you're —
20   ANNE: Oh, please. Both of you. Jack, Trish's tired. It was a
21   long trip. She didn't mean —
22   JACK: That's right. Stick up for her. Help it along. You
23   probably feel the same way.
24   TRISH: Anne, I told you that night of Cora's party. And you
25   compared *him* to Clyde Alexander. Which reminds me,
26   darling, Clyde brought your last letter over for me to
27   read. It was —
28   JACK: Thought you weren't writing to Alexander anymore?
29   ANNE: Clyde's a good friend of mine, Jack. Regardless of the
30   way we feel —
31   JACK: You lied to me, Anne.
32   ANNE: I didn't lie to you. I never lie to anyone. I may joke
33   about it, but — I said I was writing him about the two of
34   us —
35   JACK: That should have ended it. Only maybe that isn't the

1   way the rich do things. They have two of everything.

2 TRISH: Anne, the man's obviously mad —

3 ANNE: Keep out of this, Trish. This is between Jack and me.

4 JACK: Not a chance. If you think I'm tagging after you two —

5   take the crumbs when Alexander doesn't want them —

6   listening to that screwball sister moan. Tell her there's

7   an economic crunch in the country when you haven't

8   anything else to do. That those "dreadful" people on that

9   train were all going somewhere, too, even if they did have

10   to use *her* train. Only stay away from me when you're

11   doing it. I'm fussy about my company — fussier about my

12   girl. I want people who can talk my language. And I know

13   where I can find them. So long.

14 TRISH: *(After a terrible pause.)* Anne, I never meant — not that

15   you wouldn't be better off — but he'll be back.

16 ANNE: *(Ruefully)* Will he, Trish? Do you think he will? *(Blackout)*

17

18

19

20

21

22

23

24

25

26

27

28

29

30

31

32

33

34

35

Something Borrowed, Something Blue

Cast of Characters

ELLEN KISTLER

*About 21, with a charming voice; sweet,
pleasant, nice-looking, with a touch of
efficiency. Down-to-earth quality.*

MOMMA KISTLER

*50, fluttery, has a new scheme a minute.
Loves Ellen and is proud of her.*

JEFF CARTER

*A hustler, 25, miserly, conservative. In love
with Ellen; loves to make a "deal."*

1   *AT RISE:*   ELLEN KISTLER's bedroom. Middle-class furnishings.

2   ELLEN is trying to close her suitcase which is on the bed. She

3   is excited and happy to be on her way to spend her vacation in

4   Florida. MOMMA is also going.

5

6   **ELLEN:** *(Calling)* **Mom! Mom! Can you come here a minute?**

7   **MOMMA:** *(Off)* **What is it, Ellen?**

8   **ELLEN:** **I need you to sit on my suitcase. It won't close.**

9   **MOMMA:** *(Off)* **I can't now, darling. I'm testing something.**

10   **ELLEN:** *(Calling)* **And where did you put my bathing suit?**

11   **I can't go to Florida without a —** *(ELLEN breaks off abruptly*

12   *as MOMMA enters with a beach umbrella which she is opening*

13   *and closing.)* **Where did you get that thing?**

14   **MOMMA:** **I borrowed it — from the man who runs the**

15   **swimming pool.**

16   **ELLEN:** **Well, you're not taking that to Florida. We're not**

17   **traveling with a beach umbrella.**

18   **MOMMA:** **I'm going to close it.**

19   **ELLEN:** **Why do you always have to be borrowing something?**

20   **MOMMA:** **Now, Ellen —**

21   **ELLEN:** **I looked at your clothes. You haven't packed a thing.**

22   **MOMMA:** **I'm waiting for Jeff.** *(Demonstrating umbrella)* **See,**

23   **Ellen, it sort of has three speeds — all the way up — then**

24   **about halfway up — then —**

25   **ELLEN:** **What do you mean, you're waiting for Jeff?**

26   **MOMMA:** **He's bringing me a trunk. The woman he's getting**

27   **it from won't be back until this morning — from wherever**

28   **she was. I don't think that's very considerate.**

29   **ELLEN:** *(Frantically)* **Oh, we'll never get going. I know we**

30   **won't. The two weeks'll be over, and I'll be sitting here —**

31   **watching you opening and closing a beach umbrella.**

32   **MOMMA:** **Now, don't get excited, dear. Anyway, two weeks**

33   **isn't enough. You work hard in that hospital laboratory**

34   **all year long.**

35   **ELLEN:** **Look, Mom, I was lucky to get this. Some of the other**

1	workers are only getting a week's vacation.
2	MOMMA: Some of the others aren't supervisors who haven't
3	missed a day's work in two years, either. *(Doorbell rings.)*
4	There. That's probably Jeff now. The darling boy. Don't
5	forget to ask him if he got me the golf clubs.
6	ELLEN: Of course I won't. *(Take)* **What golf clubs? You don't**
7	**play golf.**
8	MOMMA: *(Going off)* **I know. But they look so chic to travel**
9	**with. Be back in a minute, darling.**
10	ELLEN: **Now, don't go wandering off again.** *(Calls)* **Do you**
11	**hear?** *(Door opens. JEFF enters, staggering under the load of*
12	*a set of golf clubs, a small trunk, a fur stole, and a surfboard.)*
13	JEFF: *(Descending scale)* **Hello. Hello. Hello. Jeff Carter's**
14	**Moving Van at your service.** *(JEFF pushes door closed with*
15	*a backward motion of his foot.)*
16	ELLEN: **My heavens, what's all this?**
17	JEFF: *(Trunk falls to floor.)* **That's the trunk. And look what**
18	**else I got: golf clubs, Aunt Tillie's summer fur, collapsible**
19	**surfboard. Had a little trouble borrowing that. And the**
20	**golf balls have a few cuts in them.**
21	ELLEN: **Jeff, I've been trying to break her of this borrowing**
22	**habit. You just encourage it.**
23	JEFF: **She has to make a** *show,* **doesn't she? Who'll know it**
24	**doesn't belong to her? Besides, look at the money she**
25	**saves.**
26	ELLEN: **But it's so fake. I hate fakery. She doesn't need any**
27	**of it.**
28	JEFF: **She needs it as much as you need this trip. Ellen, I**
29	**think you're just throwing your money away on**
30	**foolishness.**
31	ELLEN: **Now, let's not go through that again. I'm going to**
32	**Orlando. See Disney World. Relax.**
33	JEFF: **Couldn't you relax at the girls "Y" or something? Then**
34	**we could see each other at night. Save money all the way**
35	**around.**

1　ELLEN:　I don't want to save money all the way around. I
2　　　　want to get away.
3　JEFF:　You're not going to forget we're engaged once you get
4　　　　to Orlando, are you, Ellen?
5　ELLEN:　Jeff, I know you helped me get my job. And I'm
6　　　　grateful for all you've done for Mother and me, but —
7　JEFF:　Guess you don't like it because I never gave you a ring.
8　　　　That jeweler I know wouldn't let me have one at the
9　　　　wholesale price.
10　ELLEN:　If you really want to get one that badly, what's wrong
11　　　　with just buying it in a store — like everyone else?
12　JEFF:　I'm saving up for when we're older.
13　ELLEN:　Well, I guess you have something there.
14　JEFF:　And you be careful, Ellen. Remember, Disney World is
15　　　　a vacation town. You know what those vacation towns
16　　　　are like.
17　ELLEN:　I'll remember, Jeff.
18　JEFF:　Oh, I almost forgot. I have a little something for you
19　　　　for on the plane. Here you are. *(He hands her a book.)*
20　ELLEN:　*(Surprised, but doing her best.)* **A book. How nice, Jeff.**
21　　　　*(Reading the title)* **"A Handy Guide for the Young Girl Who**
22　　　　**Is About to Make a Plane Trip." It's just what I needed.**
23　　　　*(Blackout)*
24　　　　*(Their condo in Orlando. The furniture is adequate. ELLEN is*
25　　　　*bustling about. MOMMA is sitting on a chair that rocks*
26　　　　*unevenly.)*
27　MOMMA:　**Oh, I just love this condo, Ellen. Right by the shore**
28　　　　**and everything. Just think, we've been here two days**
29　　　　**already.**
30　ELLEN:　*(Lazily)* **It is wonderful, isn't it?**
31　MOMMA:　**All except this one kitchen chair. I'm half afraid to**
32　　　　**sit on it, it wiggles so.**
33　ELLEN:　*(Examines chair.)* **Well, for starters, one leg's too**
34　　　　**short.**
35　MOMMA:　**It needs something to prop it up. A book would do**

1	it. Except who'd bring a book with her on a vacation to
2	Florida?
3	ELLEN: Me. I have just the book, matter of fact. I always
4	travel prepared.
5	MOMMA: Well, I wish I could say the same thing. I have a
6	definite feeling I've forgotten something.
7	ELLEN: Too late now.
8	MOMMA: Well, maybe I didn't. I always have those moments.
9	Now, when you're ready to go downtown, dear, I have a
10	list of things we need.
11	ELLEN: Oh, dear. *(Then enthusiastically)* OK, let's have it.
12	*(Reads list MOMMA hands her.)* Sugar, coffee, vegetables,
13	sliced ham, cheese. I'll need one of your traveler's checks
14	for all this. I'm a little short of "ready," as they call it.
15	MOMMA: One of the traveler's checks. Yes. *(There is a long*
16	*pause. ELLEN looks at MOMMA. MOMMA looks to the left,*
17	*then right, then gives a silly little laugh.)*
18	ELLEN: Why did you say it that way?
19	MOMMA: What — way?
20	ELLEN: You know what way.
21	MOMMA: You probably think I forgot them. Admit it. That's
22	what you think. *(ELLEN waits.)* All right. I forgot them.
23	ELLEN: You know, it's hard to believe.
24	MOMMA: *(With great dignity)* I am *not* the first person in the
25	world to forget something, Missy.
26	ELLEN: You brought golf clubs, and you don't play golf. You
27	brought a surfboard and you haven't been near the water.
28	You have a beach umbrella that won't go up, and a trunk
29	that leaks water. Did you forget any of them? Never. You
30	forgot the one thing that makes the engine go. The
31	traveler's checks.
32	MOMMA: Well, it isn't the end of the world.
33	ELLEN: *(Recovers quickly.)* I know. So — give me the numbers.
34	That man on television — you know, the one with the
35	nose — he said if you lose your checks, all you have to do

1	is go to the office and tell them, then you give them the
2	numbers, then —
3	MOMMA: The numbers.
4	ELLEN: You don't have them either. I know you don't.
5	MOMMA: *(Brazenly)* If I don't, it's your fault!
6	ELLEN: My fault!
7	MOMMA: Trusting me. You know I'm unreliable.
8	ELLEN: Well, I can't argue with you there. But what are we
9	going to do?
10	MOMMA: Well — we'll have to borrow some.
11	ELLEN: *(Groaning)* Oh, my word. You can't borrow a traveler's
12	check. It doesn't make sense.
13	MOMMA: Why not? Your Uncle Shane lives down here
14	someplace.
15	ELLEN: Uncle Shane! We haven't talked to Uncle Shane in
16	twenty years. Besides which, he isn't even my uncle. He's
17	a friend I called "uncle."
18	MOMMA: He's practically an uncle. And stop complaining.
19	I'll call him if you don't want to.
20	ELLEN: Where?
21	MOMMA: Well, although you think I'm completely
22	incompetent —
23	ELLEN: Oh, Mother —
24	MOMMA: Don't explain.
25	ELLEN: I wasn't going to. Apparently you remembered to
26	bring your address book.
27	MOMMA: *(Gets address book from suitcase.)* Was there ever a
28	doubt?
29	ELLEN: It makes sense.
30	MOMMA: What, sweetheart?
31	ELLEN: Bringing the address book.
32	MOMMA: Don't look so dismal, Ellen. Borrowing things is a
33	perfectly charming way to meet people. I know! *(Blackout)*
34	
35

Watch Your Step

Cast of Characters

BEN WANNAMAKER

A lovable, accident-prone guy of 25 who is so nice, you forgive him for being such a klutz.

TRUDY KENNICOTT

24, pretty. Has the world at her feet including a rich daddy, so she's sincere and a "fluff" both, on occasion. Likeable.

JOE BARNER

28, and basically a "no goodnik" but with some redeeming qualities, too. A fast-talking hustler. This character must be believable so the actor is warned of over-playing.

WILLIAM KENNICOTT

Trudy's father, about 50. A very successful businessman; a bit eccentric and fussy.

1 *AT RISE:* The Kennicott library. Traditional furniture, old,
2 lived-in and comfortable. JOE BARNER and TRUDY are
3 talking. He is trying to convince her of something. She is trying
4 to say no gracefully.
5
6 TRUDY: But, Joe, I've already promised Ben I'd go to the
7 concert with him.
8 JOE: How can you talk about that drip when I'm around,
9 Trudy?
10 TRUDY: Because I'm very fond of Ben. And he's not a drip.
11 JOE: Look, you're just inviting trouble hanging around that
12 guy. He won't show up for the concert. He'll probably
13 have a case of fallen elbows or something.
14 TRUDY: Now, stop it, Joe. Ben is sweet. He really is — and he
15 can't help it if all those peculiar things happen to him.
16 JOE: Go on. Anyone who has all the accidents he does must
17 enjoy them. Look at him. He works for an insurance
18 company.
19 TRUDY: The same company you work for, incidentally, Mr.
20 Barner.
21 JOE: That's what I mean. He's giving the firm a bad name.
22 Whoever heard of an insurance agent who had two
23 broken legs in six months, a fire in his house, a tree fall
24 on him, a dog bite him in the — well, a dog bite, a hole
25 the size of a grapefruit burned in his overcoat —
26 TRUDY: Someone else chopped down that tree.
27 JOE: Yeah, but who does it always fall on? It falls on Ben
28 Wannamaker.
29 TRUDY: He broke his leg trying to pick up that old lady
30 who'd fallen on the icy pavement. And the time the dog
31 bit him, it was chasing a tramp, and Ben tried to stop
32 him. And it was *your* cigarette that ...
33 JOE: *(Cutting in)* Now, take me, on the other hand.
34 TRUDY: I thought someone did take you, Joe. Lucy's going
35 to get awfully jealous if you keep hanging around me. She

1	won't type any more letters for you. And I'd hate to break
2	up an office romance . . .
3	JOE: Don't you worry about Lucy. I can handle her in the
4	office and out of it, too. Right now, I'm concentrating on
5	you. And I've got something to match that charm bracelet
6	I gave you.
7	TRUDY: Sorry, Joe. Here comes Ben now.
8	BEN: *(Enters, nursing a sore shoulder; rubbing it.)* **Gosh, Trudy,**
9	**I'm — I'm awfully sorry I'm late. I was trying to talk to**
10	**your father and —**
11	JOE: Hey, is your father here tonight, Trudy? Where is he?
12	BEN: He was in the living room when I — I — *(Sneezes)*
13	Excuse me. When I was —
14	JOE: Never mind, Junior. That's all I want to know. See you
15	kids later.
16	BEN: Gosh, he didn't let me finish. Your father's talking to
17	Senator Klinger. He can't interrupt him.
18	TRUDY: I wish he would. And I wish Dad would sit all over
19	him. I'd like to see that conceited Mr. Me taken down a
20	couple of pegs. Come on, Ben. Let's go. The concert starts
21	at eight.
22	BEN: Well, I — I can't drive right now, Trudy.
23	TRUDY: Why can't you?
24	BEN: That's what I started to tell you. You see, I was trying to
25	sneak down the stairs so I could head your father off
26	before he could get to the living room and — and —
27	*(Sneezing)* Oh, excuse me.
28	TRUDY: And?
29	BEN: And then I tripped on the last step and my trick
30	shoulder popped out. It took me almost half an hour to
31	put it back in.
32	TRUDY: Oh, Ben, darling, does it hurt?
33	BEN: No, it's all right now. Only I couldn't stop your father
34	with it sticking out so funny and — and — *(Sneezes)*
35	Excuse me.

1   TRUDY: Are you catching cold?

2   BEN: Gosh, I hope not. Your father's awfully funny about

3   talking to people with colds.

4   TRUDY: Funny! The man has a positive phobia about it. And

5   I wanted you to make a good impression on him tonight.

6   BEN: Gosh, so did I. But do you think it'll be any use, Trudy?

7   I want to get that contract to insure his fleet of trucks,

8   but I'm afraid Joe'll beat me to it. The way he does in

9   everything else. He's the lucky one.

10   TRUDY: He's not lucky. He's noisy. And he's not going to sell

11   Dad that insurance. Now, come along with me.

12   BEN: Why? Where — where are we going?

13   TRUDY: We're going to the living room after Dad.

14   BEN: But Senator Klinger is —

15   TRUDY: I'll get rid of Senator Klinger. Then you go in and

16   talk with Dad. And put the pressure on him, Ben. Joe told

17   me if he gets Dad's contract, he'll have a chance at the

18   management of your firm.

19   BEN: That's right. I would too.

20   TRUDY: Then go after it. Oh, Ben, you're the dearest fellow I

21   know — but do you always have to let everyone else push

22   you around? You can get that contract if you try.

23   BEN: Gosh, Trudy, wouldn't that be wonderful? If I did, then

24   maybe I could ask you — I mean, maybe I could tell you —

25   *(Low)* how much you mean to me — how crazy I am about

26   you —

27   TRUDY: I wish you'd say that right out loud once — now you

28   wait here. I'll go in first and clear the path. And, Ben —

29   BEN: *(Sneezes)* Oh, excuse me.

30   TRUDY: It'll only take me a minute. Don't throw your

31   shoulder out of joint before I get back. And stop that

32   sneezing!

33   BEN: Yes, Trudy. *(Sneezes. Blackout.)*

34   *(The Kennicott living room. It is a pleasant, comfortable room.)*

35   BEN: *(Fading in)* So you see, Mr. Kennicott, if you'd let me

1	handle that insurance contract for your company, I could
2	get you a special rate that would include — *(Starts to*
3	*sneeze.)* **ah — ah —**

MR. K.: What's the matter with you, young man?

BEN: Just a little nose tickle. *(Laughs)* It's gone. Now, where was I—

MR. K.: At the special rate.

BEN: That's right. I'll get you a special rate that'll cover property damage, collision, fire, theft, floods and tornadoes.

MR. K.: Whoever heard of a tornado in Coaldale?

BEN: You can never tell, Mr. Kennicott.

MR. K.: Well, I'll tell you, Ben. I've decided to give my business to your firm. Only this is a big deal. Of course, Trudy's been plugging for you, but she doesn't understand the amount of business that's involved.

BEN: Trudy's a great gal, Mr. Kennicott. She — she — *(Sneezes)* Oh, excuse me.

MR. K.: Here, you're not catching cold, are you? Don't stand so close to me.

BEN: Oh, no, I'm not getting a cold. That was just another tickle. Dust. It's in the air.

MR. K.: If there's one thing that makes me nervous, it's people who go around spreading germs. They have no consideration. No consideration for anyone else.

BEN: Oh, you're right. I think you're perfectly right. *(Knock on door. MR. K. crosses to open it. JOE walks in.)*

JOE: Well. Well. Hello, Mr. Kennicott. You remember me? Joe Barner — Pacific Insurance Company. The smartest little insurance agent in Coaldale.

MR. K.: Oh, yes, Mr. Barner.

JOE: Hello, Ben. You here, too? You're just wasting your time, boy — just wasting your time.

BEN: Now, wait a second, Joe. I was talking to Mr. Kennicott and — and — *(Sneezes)*

1	JOE:	Say, what's wrong with you? You've been sneezing all
2		night.
3	MR. K.:	*(Upset)* He has? Why, he told me —
4	BEN:	I have not. It's only a little dust. *(Sneezes)*
5	JOE:	Look at his eyes. They're all red. And his nose is all red.
6		*(Alert)* Say, didn't you call on the McDonnell's this
7		afternoon after you left the office?
8	BEN:	Well, yes. I wanted to see how Mr. McDonnell is doing.
9		He had a heart attack and — I took his wife some
10		vegetable soup my mother made. Why?
11	JOE:	Mr. Kennicott, did you ever hear of Typhoid Mary?
12	MR. K.:	Certainly.
13	JOE:	Then take a look at her first cousin, Ben here. Didn't
14		you know that all the McDonnell children have measles?
15		*(Blackout)*
16		*(BEN's bedroom. He is sitting on a rocker in a flannel robe.)*
17	BEN:	Gosh, Trudy, do you think you should have come to see
18		me?
19	TRUDY:	It's all right, Ben. The doctor said I couldn't catch
20		measles after the tenth day.
21	BEN:	How does your — your Dad feel?
22	TRUDY:	Oh, Ben, honestly. If you have to take vegetable
23		soup to your sick clients, can't you make sure their
24		children don't have measles? And if you had to get
25		measles, couldn't you have had them by yourself? Why'd
26		you have to give them to Dad?
27	BEN:	Well, I didn't mean to. Is he — is he still so angry?
28	TRUDY:	He thinks you're a menace to the community.
29	BEN:	Well, no, I'm not. I'm —
30	TRUDY:	Everything's in such a mess, Ben. Dad swears he
31		won't give you his insurance business. And — and he says
32		if you come within fifty yards of the house, he'll turn the
33		dogs loose.
34	BEN:	But — but that isn't going to make any difference between
35		— between you and me, is it, Trudy? *(No answer.)* Trudy?

1   TRUDY: Ben, I don't know what to say.

2   BEN: But Trudy, you can't turn me down — not when I'm just

3   getting over the measles.

4   TRUDY: Ben, is there any use in going on? If I married you,

5   I'd be a widow in six months. If I lived that long.

6   BEN: Yeah, but it would be kind of a nice six months.

7   TRUDY: For a while there, I thought things were going to be

8   different. Hardly anything happened to you. But it

9   always ends up the same way. You try to do something

10   nice for somebody, and get hit by a truck — or something.

11   BEN: It isn't that I don't try, Trudy.

12   TRUDY: Oh, Ben, darling, I know you try. And you're sweet

13   — and you're thoughtful. But — that's what makes it all

14   so — so —

15   BEN: Don't feel sorry for me.

16   TRUDY: But I do. And Ben, that isn't good. You've got to pull

17   yourself together — trick shoulder and all. You've got to

18   sell Dad that policy. You've got to prove to me you can

19   do it. Once and for all.

20   BEN: *(Bravely determined)* All right, by gosh, I will.

21   TRUDY: Now, you come out to the house tomorrow night, and —

22   BEN: But I thought you said — I mean — the dogs —

23   TRUDY: I'll handle the dogs. You just get to the house and

24   talk to him. If you manage to do that all in one piece, I

25   think you'll have a second chance at convincing him. But,

26   Ben, if anything happens to you between now and then,

27   so help me, I'll never speak to you again as long as I live.

28   BEN: Trudy, you're so sweet. No wonder I'm in love with you.

29   TRUDY: I'm not sweet. I wish I were. Right now all I am is

30   desperate. *(Blackout)*

31

32

33

34

35

Trade-Off

Cast of Characters

NORA COLBY
*Age 39, pretty but harassed. She is timid,
uncertain, tentative in her approach, and only
wants the best for her husband, John.*

JOHN COLBY
*An honest, caring lawyer, 44. Straight-arrow,
kind, concerned; has a genuine regard for his
clients and friends.*

ED JOHNSON
*Ed is a smooth-talking, 60-year-old lawyer
with connections and favors he can "call in"
when needed. He is a behind-the-scenes
politician.*

MRS. MANZINI
A 50-year-old woman with an Italian accent.

1	*AT RISE:* JOHN COLBY's law offices are a shade tacky, worn and
2	out-of-date. We can hear a typewriter clacking in the outer
3	room. JOHN doesn't have a wealthy clientele — more on the
4	bottom of the socio-economic scale. JOHN has a pleasant,
5	reassuring manner. ED JOHNSON, his guest entering the door,
6	has an air of hustle about him.
7	
8	**JOHN: Come in. Come in, Ed. Sit down.**
9	**ED: Thanks, John. How are things?**
10	**JOHN: Well —** *(Makes a so-so gesture with his hands.)* **More to the**
11	**point, how is your law practice these days?**
12	**ED: Well, about like yours. Good one day, then bad the next.**
13	**JOHN: Now, that's the big politician talking. Never let**
14	**yourself be pinned down. What's on your mind?**
15	**ED: I hear your practice is OK, but — you're barely scraping**
16	**by financially. You're foolish, John.**
17	**JOHN: Maybe. Maybe that's the best I'm going to do.**
18	**ED: I hear you turned down the appointment to act for the**
19	**county in those tax foreclosures out Greenvale way.**
20	**JOHN: Those people are my friends.**
21	**ED: Could be that you don't know who your real friends are.**
22	**Sometimes a man can be too good for his own good.**
23	**JOHN: That's one way of looking at it.**
24	**ED: And the Shellhammer divorce case. You convinced them**
25	**they ought to get together and kissed a nice fat fee**
26	**goodbye.**
27	**JOHN: They didn't really want a divorce. They're pretty**
28	**happy being back together again.**
29	**ED: I thought you quit the Boy Scouts when your voice**
30	**changed.**
31	**JOHN: Ed, I'm not out to make a fortune.**
32	**ED: Then maybe you won't be interested in my proposition.**
33	**JOHN: Oh, I couldn't say I wouldn't listen. Go ahead.**
34	**ED: Well, it's like this. I've been keeping an eye on you for**
35	**some time. So have a lot of other people. State Senator**

1		Gillespie, for instance.
2	JOHN:	That's very flattering.
3	ED:	And I'm so busy in politics that I'm going to have to turn
4		over most of my legal work to another lawyer. I was
5		thinking of you.
6	JOHN:	I see.
7	ED:	A good deal of it would be private legal work for the
8		senator himself. And if he was pleased with the way you
9		handled things — well —
10	JOHN:	Well, what?
11	ED:	Did you ever happen to think that you have all the
12		qualifications for being a darned good judge?
13	JOHN:	I have thought of it. What lawyer hasn't? But I hoped
14		that maybe someday — it's just a crazy dream of mine.
15	ED:	It doesn't have to be. You know, Judge Thomas has been
16		thinking of retiring. He's nearing seventy. Almost any
17		day now, they'll be drawing up a panel of attorneys to
18		fill his place. I think you stand a good chance of getting
19		on that list, with my help — and with the senator's
20		influence behind you — you'd probably be appointed.
21	JOHN:	*(Dazed)* Ed, you're kidding!
22	ED:	You try us and see.
23	JOHN:	But — but — You don't know how much it would
24		mean to me. I can't even begin to tell you.
25	ED:	Sure. I know. But you've got what it takes, John — all
26		you need to do is steer it into the right channels.
27	JOHN:	You sound a little like my wife, Nora. She talks that
28		way sometimes.
29	ED:	Your wife's a right smart woman. Yes, sir. A mighty smart
30		woman. Why just yesterday, she was out at my house,
31		and we were talking about you —
32	JOHN:	*(Sharply)* You — and my wife —
33	ED:	Sure. You know how good friends Nora and my missus
34		used to be. And I thought if I could give you a leg up —
35	JOHN:	You mean my wife asked you to do this?

1   ED: Now, John. Of course not. *(JOHN starts out to other room.)*
2   Hey, where are you going?
3   JOHN: Ed, will you excuse me?
4   ED: Yes.
5   JOHN: I've got something to attend to.
6   ED: Go ahead.
7   JOHN: Well, first I want to thank you. You've been a sincere
8   friend coming around like this. I appreciate it.
9   ED: But you will consider my proposition? You will think it
10   over?
11 JOHN: Yes, Ed. I'll think it over. *(Blackout)*
12   *(JOHN and NORA's kitchen. It is homey and warm. JOHN*
13   *comes in.)*
14 JOHN: *(Enters rapidly)* Nora. Nora, where are you?
15 NORA: *(Off camera. Comes on.)* In the living room.
16 JOHN: Come out to the kitchen a minute, honey. I want to
17   talk. *(NORA comes on.)*
18 NORA: Did you have your meeting with Ed?
19 JOHN: And what a meeting!
20 NORA: What did he want?
21 JOHN: He wanted to send some business my way. And there
22   was some talk about a judgeship which I could probably
23   get with Senator Gillespie's help.
24 NORA: It sounds absolutely marvelous.
25 JOHN: Does it?
26 NORA: Honey, of course. It's what you've always dreamed of.
27 JOHN: I suppose so. I've dreamed of a lot of things. But in the
28   middle of all those dreams, know what always pulls me
29   back to reality, Nora? *(Pause)* It's an old cliché. There's
30   no such thing as a free lunch.
31 NORA: I could have told you that.
32 JOHN: Could you? Is that why you made a "social call" — I
33   think that's what you call it — to get things set up so I'd
34   get these offers?
35 NORA: No. I made my social call — if you will — because I

1   wanted you to be a success. Not just for me, but for you.

2 JOHN: I thought I was a success.

3 NORA: Oh, John, you are.

4 JOHN: Apparently not. Not in your eyes. Why didn't you just

5   tell me to my face you thought I was a failure. It wouldn't

6   have hurt half as much.

7 NORA: I never felt that way. John, I love you. I have from the

8   day we met.

9 JOHN: I love you, too. Only all these years I thought you

10   wanted the same things I wanted. I thought we were

11   working together, loving each other . . . .

12 NORA: We were. We are. And I want you to be happy. I want

13   people to look up to you and respect you.

14 JOHN: But you thought that was best accomplished if I were

15   rich?

16 NORA: Is there anything wrong with being rich?

17 JOHN: No. Not inherently. Matter of fact, I fully subscribe to

18   the capitalistic system. What American doesn't?

19 NORA: John, I saw what Ed and Celia have and I want it for

20   us — for you, for me, and for Ellen. Instead of living the

21   way we should and could — considering the investment

22   in time and money you've made in your years of

23   schooling — in the fact that all a lawyer has to sell is his

24   time — we're practically at poverty level.

25 JOHN: Nora!

26 NORA: It's true. I pay the bills. I handle the money.

27 JOHN: You're good at figures.

28 NORA: Not when there are no figures to work with. Here's a

29   letter from Ellen we got this morning. That art school of

30   hers costs a mint. She says, "Next year will be even more

31   expensive, I'm afraid. And it's been so wonderful here.

32   But it isn't as important as all that. I don't want you or

33   Dad to worry. I don't want Dad to feel he has to work so

34   hard to keep me here . . ." I hate her to feel that way.

35 JOHN: I do, too.

1	NORA: I'll admit I tried to fix things so they'd be easier for us.
2	But, John, that's not criminal, is it?
3	JOHN: I'm sorry, honey. I guess I wanted to do it all by
4	myself. A man's ego —
5	NORA: — Is a fragile thing. I know, darling, but you know
6	what is even more fragile? An empty wallet!
7	JOHN: You're right there.
8	NORA: John, think over Ed's offer, will you?
9	JOHN: Is that what you want?
10	NORA: I want you to get that judgeship. I can't imagine any
11	words that have a nicer ring than, "The Honorable Judge
12	Colby presiding."
13	JOHN: All right, Nora. I guess you win. *(Timid knocking on*
14	*door. NORA goes to door, opens it. MRS. MANZINI in doorway.)*
15	NORA: Why, Mrs. Manzini, how nice to see you. Come in.
16	MRS. MANZINI: Forgive me. I bother you. But I must see your
17	husband. Was no in his office.
18	NORA: Yes, he's here.
19	JOHN: Good evening, Mrs. Manzini. What can I do for you?
20	MRS. MANZINI: It's my son, my Guido. He is arrest' . . . in
21	jail . . . .
22	NORA: Mrs. Manzini, how terrible.
23	JOHN: Tell us about it, Mrs. Manzini.
24	MRS. MANZINI: My Guido, you know works chauffeur. Last
25	night car get in smashup. Lady hurt bad. Other car
26	wrecked.
27	JOHN: I see. And Guido was driving?
28	MRS. MANZINI: No. No. Guido no work last night. Boss, he
29	drive. Runs away. Now he say Guido drive, Guido to
30	blame. Is no right they put Guido in jail for something
31	he did no do.
32	JOHN: No. It certainly isn't.
33	MRS. MANZINI: Please. You help my Guido, no? He need
34	help bad.
35	JOHN: I'll do what I can. If I'm satisfied that Guido is telling

1   the truth, I'll go to bat for him.
2 MRS. MANZINI: My Guido, he no lie.
3 JOHN: Was he home last night?
4 MRS. MANZINI: No. He sleep garage at boss' place.
5 JOHN: I see. And who did you say Guido worked for?
6 MRS. MANZINI: Fine family. Name Gillespie.
7 NORA: Who — who did you say?
8 MRS. MANZINI: Gillespie. His father is big man, state senator.
9 JOHN: I see.
10 NORA: Oh, John. What are you going to do?
11 JOHN: Have a talk with Guido.
12 NORA: But surely you couldn't be thinking of —
13 JOHN: If Guido's telling the truth, I've got to help him.
14   There's just one kind of law, Nora — and it's got to work
15   the same for everybody.
16 NORA: But, John — think — think what this could mean. Ed
17   Johnson and the senator — your judgeship, everything!
18 JOHN: I can't help that. Come on, Mrs. Manzini. Let's go see
19   Guido. *(They exit as we go to black.)*
20
21
22
23
24
25
26
27
28
29
30
31
32
33
34
35

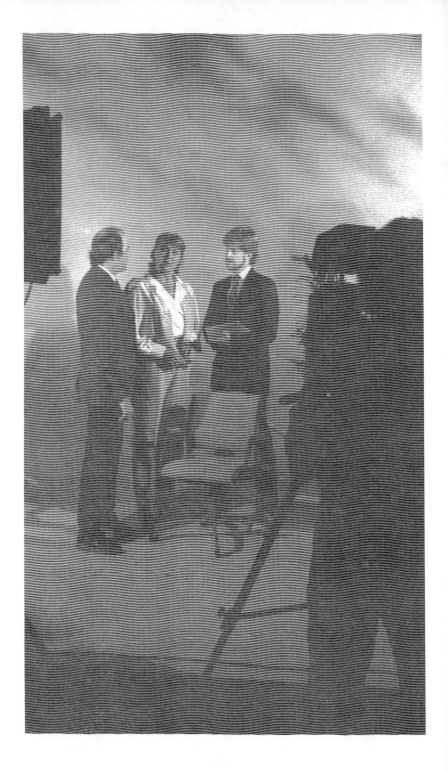

The Choice

Cast of Characters

BETH MORRISON

20, immature, pretty, lacks confidence. Very much in love with her husband; pouts if she doesn't get her own way, needs constant reassurance; yet, with it all, kind.

SANDY MORRISON

A nice guy of 26. Good-looking, practical, takes a realistic approach to life. A professional architect who loves his wife and is concerned for her.

VICTOR SANTIAGO

Hispanic, 48. Very kind, intelligent, has the harassed look of a human services worker with constant problems.

1 *AT RISE:* The scene is a fragment of a wooded area. Trees, large
2 rocks, moonlight. We hear the night sounds of the woods,
3 mysterious yet friendly. BETH and SANDY, married two days,
4 are looking at the view. They're in love and the world is
5 smiling — at the moment.
6
7 SANDY: What a great place, Beth. I'm going to make an early
8 reservation. Spend all my honeymoons here.
9 BETH: How many are you planning on, Mr. Morrison?
10 SANDY: One every six months — and all of them with you,
11 Mrs. Morrison.
12 BETH: That's the kind of talk I like. Think you could spare a
13 kiss for your favorite bride?
14 SANDY: Well, maybe a quick one. *(They kiss.)*
15 BETH: Not bad. For a quick one.
16 SANDY: We'll try a slower one later.
17 BETH: Oh, Sandy, I'm so happy. I keep thinking — something's
18 going to fall on my head — jar me back to reality and —
19 take it away from me.
20 SANDY: Hey, lady. What kind of talk is that?
21 BETH: Silly, I guess. I always worry when I don't have
22 anything to worry about.
23 SANDY: Well, for starters, you can worry about me. Am I
24 making his favorite salad? Does he like meat loaf? Should
25 I buy wash and wear or all cotton?
26 BETH: I know it's silly, honey.
27 SANDY: Not really.
28 BETH: Yes, it is. Except — I have these premonitions. I think
29 I'm a semi-witch.
30 SANDY: Semi?
31 BETH: Half wrong all the time.
32 SANDY: Come on. The law of averages gives you that much.
33 BETH: No. You know what it really is, Sandy?
34 SANDY: Nothing. You're great as is.
35 BETH: Being brought up an only child. Plus a mother who

1   was the world's last great professional mother.

2 SANDY: We'll have children someday, Bethie.

3 BETH: We certainly will. And I'm not afraid of that old cliché
4   either, Sandy. That is the biggie for any woman.

5 SANDY: I thought I was your security, Babe.

6 BETH: You are. Only when I was a youngster, all I ever wanted
7   for Christmas was a bigger, newer doll.

8 SANDY: Poor frustrated baby. Just don't forget, I'm a
9   struggling architect with the emphasis on struggling. It's
10   all I can do to pay Miss Wolfe her salary. So, if you're
11   planning a family of six, why —

12 BETH: I don't care about money where children are concerned.

13 SANDY: Look, Babe, I'm all for as many children as you
14   want. You know that. Only this is our honeymoon. We'll
15   get the family later. OK?

16 BETH: OK, darling.

17 SANDY: That's better. Now, how about the slow kiss we were
18   talking about, huh? *(Blackout)*

19   *(SANDY's office, conventional furniture, blueprints in evidence.*
20   *It is months later. BETH bursts into the office. SANDY is bent*
21   *over a drawing board.)*

22 BETH: *(She is close to tears.)* **Sandy. Oh, Sandy.**

23 SANDY: *(Looks up from working.)* **Hi, darling. Wait a second till**
24   **— oh, honey, you look awful.**

25 BETH: Sandy, I saw Dr. Loquisto this afternoon.

26 SANDY: You said. I don't care what he told you — as long as
27   you're OK.

28 BETH: That doesn't matter, Sandy, only — I'm not all right.
29   I — I'm a failure.

30 SANDY: *(Embraces her.)* **Oh, Beth, you're not a failure. You**
31   know that. We're having trouble now. All right. Everyone
32   has trouble some time or another. That's what the human
33   condition's all about.

34 BETH: But not everyone has my kind of trouble. *(Suddenly)*
35   I hate doctors.

1	SANDY: Darling, don't look like that. There are millions of
2	women who can't have children.
3	BETH: Remember, I told you I was selfish.
4	SANDY: You're not.
5	BETH: Yes, I am. I'm sorry for those millions of women, if
6	there are that many, but I'm sorriest for myself. I am. It's
7	ironic. We want a baby so badly and can't have one, and
8	there are women who don't want one, or don't want
9	another one, and they're — you know, honey — once,
10	when I was younger, I visited my cousin Danny — he's
11	the lawyer in Plainfield, New Jersey — and he had a little
12	message pasted on his mirror. It said, "Oh, Lord, if you
13	forgive my little jokes on thee, I'll forgive thy great big
14	one on me." *(Pause)* How true that was.
15	SANDY: Oh, darling, don't.
16	BETH: I just wanted a child so badly. Dammit, now it'll never
17	happen.
18	SANDY: Hey! That's not my girl.
19	BETH: He'd have closed the circle for us. Completed our
20	lives. If you only knew how I dreamed.
21	SANDY: We could adopt a child, you know.
22	BETH: Adopt?
23	SANDY: Why not?
24	BETH: Because it wouldn't be the same.
25	SANDY: Then, would you consider — now, don't get angry.
26	BETH: At what?
27	SANDY: What I'm going to suggest. Would you consider a
28	surrogate mother? Using me as the father of course.
29	BETH: A sur —
30	SANDY: Beth, I love you, and you alone. You know that.
31	BETH: I know, honey. Believe it or not, that thought crossed
32	my mind too.
33	SANDY: It did?
34	BETH: But I felt there was such a strong chance of the
35	mother backing out at the last minute. They do. Some

1	women. And then —
2	SANDY: I know.
3	BETH: It seemed so cruel to the mother, Sandy. To literally
4	take the baby, pay her the money, then say, OK, my dear,
5	thanks a million, but —
6	SANDY: There's that procedure — they do an implant.
7	BETH: Expensive beyond words. And the success rate is —
8	well, don't get your hopes up if we'd elect to try that.
9	SANDY: Which puts us back to square one, honey. How about
10	it? We want a child — and it looks like adoption is the
11	only way.
12	BETH: I know. So — *(She lifts her head. She'll lick this yet!)* OK.
13	Let's go, then. By George, Sandy, we will lick this. We
14	deserve our happiness! *(Blackout)*
15	*(An adoption agency. Like most human services offices, it is cold*
16	*looking — scarred furniture, hard chairs, a few plants sitting*
17	*around. SANDY is sitting quietly. BETH is restless, pacing,*
18	*sitting, standing.)*
19	SANDY: Beth, for Pete's sake, take it easy. We're only having
20	an interview here with Mr. — ah —
21	BETH: Santiago.
22	SANDY: Exactly. We're not walking out with a baby today.
23	BETH: Oh, Sandy, if only we were.
24	SANDY: Honey, I think we will get a child. Mr. San —
25	BETH: 'Tiago —
26	SANDY: Assured me — us — we're highly eligible. The right
27	age. I have a good profession. You have a sweet face.
28	BETH: Oh, he never said that. Did he really say that? A sweet
29	face?
30	SANDY: *(Laughs. Slowly.)* Well — he could have.
31	BETH: Oh, you and your dumb jokes. Maybe we hadn't better
32	joke about — you know, not everyone thinks your jokes
33	are that great.
34	SANDY: You always laugh.
35	BETH: That was in the marriage contract. Seriously, honey, don't.

1 SANDY: I won't. You just look so horribly worried. With that
2 I'm-about-to-jump-into-a-canyon-thirty-feet-deep-look. Come
3 on.
4 BETH: I should have stayed home. Let you handle it.
5 SANDY: Then give me heck if I'd —
6 BETH: Oh, Sandy, it wouldn't matter. A boy or a girl. That's why
7 I trimmed the room in yellow. I always said if the baby's
8 all right, that's all I — *(Suddenly)* Oh, where is he? It's
9 maddening. Our appointment was for two o'clock.
10 SANDY: It's only two-thirty.
11 BETH: He's always late. They do it to keep your anxiety high.
12 The last time — *(Suddenly the door opens and MR. SANTIAGO*
13 *comes in.)*
14 MR. SANTIAGO: Ah, Mr. and Mrs. Morrison. Please forgive
15 me for making you wait. There's always a crisis at a
16 human services agency.
17 BETH: Oh, goodness me. It was no problem, Mr. Santiago.
18 SANDY: Everything working out OK for us, Mr. Santiago?
19 MR. SANTIAGO: I believe so, Mr. Morrison. Since neither of
20 you was fussy about the sex of the child —
21 BETH: A boy or a girl.
22 MR. SANTIAGO: Makes it easier for us, of course.
23 SANDY: *(Eagerly)* Then you think —
24 MR. SANTIAGO: Yes, Mr. Morrison, I do think. We have a boy
25 — or will have —
26 BETH: Oh, a boy, Sandy. I truly hoped —
27 SANDY: We both hoped for a boy.
28 MR. SANTIAGO: He should be coming to us soon. In a week
29 or so. We're not sure.
30 BETH: Blue really is my favorite color. And I'm telling you
31 right off, Sandy, no guns or boxing gloves or —
32 MR. SANTIAGO: If only — *(Everything in the room stops. Finally:)*
33 SANDY: If only what?
34 MR. SANTIAGO: Mr. and Mrs. Morrison, we'd never discussed
35 this issue. There was no need for it before. There usually is

1   no need. We are often able to match couples almost
2   perfectly with the children we get — race,
3   characteristics, even religion — Catholic babies with
4   Catholic families. Jewish babies with Jewish families.
5   SANDY: Religion would be no barrier.
6   BETH: No, none at all.
7   MR. SANTIAGO: The baby I'm talking about is bi-racial, Mrs.
8   Morrison.
9   BETH: *(Stunned)* Bi —
10 MR. SANTIAGO: The offspring of a white mother and a black
11   father. The child is light brown in color. A dear little
12   fellow. Three weeks old. But he has the characteristics
13   of a black infant. Dark, tight, curly hair, brown skin,
14   brown eyes. There would be no mistaking the child for —
15 SANDY: *(Turns to BETH.)* We hadn't thought —
16 BETH: *(She is floored.)* A bi-racial baby. *(Dazed)* We — I don't
17   mean — I don't want to say the wrong thing. We thought
18   we'd be getting — I just assumed — I never figured it
19   wouldn't be a child of my — our race.
20 MR. SANTIAGO: I understand.
21 BETH: We're not racists, Mr. Santiago. Truly, I've worked
22   with — Sandy employs two black men in his office who
23   are — the thing is I hadn't thought about — to raise a
24   bi-racial baby —
25 MR. SANTIAGO: I understand, and we don't need your
26   decision today, Mrs. Morrison. No. Please, understand.
27   You think it over. Take a week. Take two weeks if
28   necessary. I assure you — *(BETH puts her hands to her face.*
29   *What can she say?)*
30 SANDY: Beth!
31 BETH: No. It isn't fair! What are we going to do? Oh, Sandy,
32   what? *(Blackout)*
33
34
35

Trouble with the Third Party

Cast of Characters

KATHY VAN ZANT

A charming, personable wife and business partner. Honest and loving. Wants the best for her husband's writing career.

STEVE VAN ZANT

Her husband and business partner. Age 35. Handsome, quick to argue, a writer as well as a book store owner. Indulgent and susceptible to flattery.

RITA COLLINS

She's really not a bad sort. Affected, yes, but she really likes Steve, is nearly forty, and running a little scared of ever marrying. It is important that while this character comes off sticky, she must not be caricatured.

1	*AT RISE:*	Fragment of a book store. A few book racks, counter,
2		cash register and telephone. KATHY is organizing counter for
3		the day's business. STEVE approaches her from behind and
4		puts a caring hand on KATHY's shoulder. She turns.
5		
6	STEVE:	**Darling, I'm sorry. I don't know what started me off**
7		**this morning. I wouldn't change a single thing about you.**
8	KATHY:	**It was my fault, Steve. The coffee really was awful.**
9	STEVE:	**The coffee was fine.**
10	KATHY:	**It was cold. And it was horrible.**
11	STEVE:	*(Gives her a big hug and a kiss.)* **Are you trying to tell me**
12		**I don't know a good cup of coffee when I taste one?**
13	KATHY:	**Steve — for heaven's sake! It's time to open the shop.**
14	STEVE:	**What of it? Nobody ever expects a book store to open**
15		**on time.** *(Clock strikes nine.)* **Holy smokes! Nine o'clock.**
16		**OK, I'll unlock the door.** *(STEVE exits. Blackout.)*
17		*(STEVE is pecking away at the typewriter. After a wild burst,*
18		*he sits back, pulls the page from the typewriter with a grandiose*
19		*gesture, reads, then obviously pleased, calls for KATHY.)*
20	STEVE:	*(Calling)* **Kathy. Kathy. Can you come out here a**
21		**second?**
22	KATHY:	*(Off)* **I'm arranging the "Bobsey Twins." This children's**
23		**section is a mess. What is it?**
24	STEVE:	**I want you to read this last chapter of my book. I just**
25		**finished it.**
26	KATHY:	*(Comes on, dust cloth in hand, a strand of hair flopping*
27		*over one eye.)* **Why do you always wait until I'm on the**
28		**stepladder? Or else waiting on a customer.**
29	STEVE:	**Look at this. I think it's tremendous.**
30	KATHY:	*(Reads quickly.)* **Hmmm.** *(Pause. STEVE looks expectant.)*
31		**I see you've gone back to calling your heroine Cindy Lou again.**
32	STEVE:	**What's the matter with the name Cindy Lou? It**
33		**expressed just the feeling of the deep south I want to**
34		**get . . . .**
35	KATHY:	**It sounds a little cheap to me.**

1	STEVE: That's because it's simple and sincere. You wouldn't
2	understand it.
3	KATHY: Simple and sincere, like your dear and good friend,
4	Rita Collins, who talked you into it.
5	STEVE: At least Rita offers constructive criticism. She doesn't
6	harp at me all the time.
7	KATHY: Then why don't you give her the chapter to read?
8	STEVE: Look, are you going to read the chapter, or are you
9	going to stand around all morning belittling Rita Collins?
10	*(Sound — bell tinkles — door opens, Off.)*
11	KATHY: All right. I'll read it. You wait on whoever that is and
12	see if you can't manage to sell a copy of that president's
13	awful memoirs. We're stuck with tons of them. *(Door*
14	*closing. Bell tinkles again. High heels tapping on floor.)* **I'll take**
15	this in the back. There's the customer. *(KATHY dashes off*
16	*with manuscript.)*
17	RITA: *(Off, coming on calling. Holds package, wrapped.)* **Yoo-hoo.**
18	Steve, it's me!
19	STEVE: *(Straightens tie. Sees hair is in place with hand movement.*
20	*Lights up.)* **Oh, good morning, Rita.**
21	RITA: I was just passing the store and I thought to myself, I'll
22	just pop in and see how dear Stephen is. And dear
23	Katherine, too, of course.
24	STEVE: Well, thanks very much.
25	RITA: And I did so want to show you this. *(Unwraps package.*
26	*It is an ugly vase of sorts.)*
27	STEVE: *(Examines it doubtfully.)* **What — what is it?**
28	RITA: Why, Steve! It's a pottery vase. A talented, little friend
29	of mine over in Greenvale makes them. Isn't it a perfect
30	duck?
31	STEVE: What do you do with it?
32	RITA: You make simply sweet floral arrangements in it. And
33	so many book stores are widening their spheres these
34	days. I thought it would be perfectly splendid if you put
35	in a line of these. There's no telling what sort of customers

1   they'd attract.

2   STEVE: No, there isn't, is there? Look, Rita, I'm sorry, and I
3   know you're trying to be helpful, but this is a book store —
4   and I hardly think that this is the kind of thing that
5   would —

6   KATHY: *(Comes back on holding manuscript.)* Oh, Steve, I've
7   read the chapter, and I honestly don't think — oh — oh,
8   the itch is in again. Good morning, Rita.

9   RITA: Good morning, Kathy, dear. What were you saying?

10   KATHY: It can wait.

11   STEVE: No, go ahead. Get it off your chest. I want Rita to hear.
12   After all, she's been very helpful with the book.

13   KATHY: Yes, I can see her fine English hand in almost every
14   line.

15   RITA: Oh, dear, Steve. Kathy doesn't like it.

16   STEVE: Go ahead, Kathy. Let's have a display of your fine
17   critical powers.

18   KATHY: I don't mean to criticize, Steve, but — well, this just
19   isn't you. It's not like anything you've ever written before.
20   It's — it's so heavy-handed, so fake . . . .

21   RITA: Steve felt he wanted to do something better than those
22   frivolous little magazine pieces.

23   KATHY: But that's where Steve's real talent lies.

24   STEVE: Implying that I'm too moronic to tackle a sound and
25   serious piece of work.

26   KATHY: This is neither sound nor serious. Darling, that scene
27   where Cindy Lou says goodbye to Billy Bob — it's simply
28   ludicrous.

29   RITA: Take heart, Steve. Sometimes it's the ones who love us
30   most who quite innocently try to hold us back.

31   KATHY: Oh, keep out of this, you — you marshmallow!

32   STEVE: Kathy! That's hardly very polite.

33   KATHY: I know. Excuse it, Rita.

34   STEVE: Rita has been helpful. Certainly *you* haven't given
35   me much encouragement.

1   KATHY: Because it's so wrong, Steve. After all, we do sell
2   books here. We should try and keep the level of literacy
3   up — not perpetrate pieces of sticky junk like this on an
4   unsuspecting public — if you'd ever get it published —
5   which I doubt.
6   STEVE: Junk, is it?
7   KATHY: That's exactly what it is — perfumed, pretentious
8   junk! And you can thank Rita for that!
9   STEVE: And there's something else we can thank Rita for —
10   this! *(He displays the avant-garde piece of pottery RITA has*
11   *brought in.)*
12   KATHY: Great Scott, what is it?
13   STEVE: It's pottery. And we're going to put in a whole line of it.
14   KATHY: Of all the ridiculous — ideas. This is a book store.
15   STEVE: Well, drugstores sell bathing caps, automobile tires
16   and bagels. We're going to expand too. No telling what
17   sort of customers we'll attract with pottery and — and
18   greeting cards.
19   KATHY: Ye Frightful Old Gift Shop-pe. Over my dead body.
20   STEVE: If we can't do it any other way.
21   KATHY: Stephen Van Zant, you must be out of your mind! Let
22   me out of here!
23   STEVE: Nobody's stopping you! Where are you going?
24   KATHY: Home to take a bath. I want to get the smell of lavender
25   and old cinnamon buns off me. Goodbye, Rita. Happy
26   hunting. *(She flounces off, high heels clicking on floor. Door opens.*
27   *Bell tinkles. Door slams.)*
28   STEVE: Kathy — come back here!
29   RITA: Oh, dear. I'm afraid I've been the unwitting cause of a tiff,
30   haven't I? *(Blackout)*
31
32
33
34
35

The Road Back

Cast of Characters

LAURA CORRIGAN

A high-strung, emotional woman of 30 who has gone through a shattering tragedy, cross-addiction (drugs and alcohol), and has seen her husband walk out on her.

CORNELIUS "NEELY" SHAMBACH

A black man, age 19, who is also a recovering addict, Laura's AA sponsor, and an immensely likeable and supportive man. (A white man can also play this role.)

1	*AT RISE:* The interior of LAURA CORRIGAN's home. She is not
2	a good housekeeper. She is phoning her mother from her kitchen
3	which has a rocker and a sofa as well as other equipment. The
4	time is seven-thirty p.m. The locale is a semi-large U.S. eastern
5	city.
6	
7	LAURA: *(Phoning)* **Hey, Momma, how's the kid? . . . Oh, come**
8	**on. Everyone over forty has arthritis . . . I could name**
9	**doctors who . . . Just kidding . . . Don't get upset.**
10	**Honestly. Listen, hold it a minute, will you . . . Just**
11	**getting a bottle of wine handy in case . . .** *(She sets down*
12	*telephone receiver and takes a bottle of wine from the shelf, puts*
13	*it on the cupboard. Slowly:)* **No, I do not sneak a drink,**
14	**Mother. I have not had a drink, sneaked or otherwise,**
15	**for two years, and I think you have a heck of a nerve**
16	**suggesting that I do, even if you are my mother. You**
17	**know, you can go too far too, madame. I'm not fourteen**
18	**anymore and it just so happens I don't live in your home**
19	**anymore. I live in my own house, and if I can't do what**
20	**I want, then . . . No, I'm not mean. All I want is for you to**
21	**keep some of your big ideas to yourself and we'll get along**
22	**perfectly fine . . . No, I don't mean you can't come over**
23	**when you want.** *Au contraire,* **I want you to come over**
24	**whenever you want to because even if you do get pesky**
25	**at times, I get pesky too, and besides, you're my mom,**
26	**and I love you, and we're family and that's what it's all**
27	**about, isn't it? . . . Right, kid? . . . Absolutely . . . Seriously**
28	**now, Mom, try those new pain pills Dr. Jasewitz**
29	**recommended, will you? He's a terrific doctor, I hear, and**
30	**I trust him . . . Exactly . . . OK, honey, now remember,**
31	**you're coming Sunday for dinner . . . Yes, at five-thirty,**
32	**then we can talk. OK? Bye, hon. Love you.** *(She replaces*
33	*phone, looks at bottle, puts it back, waits a minute, takes it down*
34	*again, walks around kitchen, shakes the coffeepot, pours a cup,*
35	*takes deep breaths, drinks coffee, puts bottle back, takes it down*

1	*again, then starts to cry. She picks up telephone and dials again.)*
2	Neely?...Oh, thank goodness, you're home...I
3	don't know ... Neely, I haven't had a drink in almost two
4	years. You know that... Yes, I was...I was thinking of
5	having a drink. I've earned it...I mean, it's been almost
6	two years, and I can handle it now...I wouldn't think
7	of it if I couldn't handle it... You think you should? Come
8	over? Well, I tell you I can handle it, but you only live
9	five doors away from me, and if you're sure you aren't
10	too tired, we could have supper together, Neely...Yes,
11	I promise. *(Replaces telephone. She goes to mirror and fixes up,*
12	*new lipstick, combs her hair, adjusts her pantyhose. The doorbell*
13	*rings. She admits a tall, handsome black man of nineteen.*
14	*LAURA runs to him. He is NEELY SHAMBACH.)*
15	Oh, Neely. Thanks for coming. *(They take each other's*
16	*hands, possibly hug.)*
17	NEELY: Now, what's going on here, Laura Corrigan? I'm your
18	sponsor at our AA meetings, remember?
19	LAURA: And my best friend.
20	NEELY: I hope so.
21	LAURA: Oh, Neely, it's — it's that time of the year. The
22	anniversary ....
23	NEELY: I didn't know.
24	LAURA: I can't.... *(Starts to cry.)*
25	NEELY: You don't have to —
26	LAURA: Yes, I do. My beautiful daughter was taken from me
27	four years ago. *(She covers her face with her hands*
28	*momentarily.)* That horrible —
29	NEELY: Laura, look at me.
30	LAURA: No.
31	NEELY: *(Gently takes her hands from her face.)* Laura, your child
32	wasn't taken from you. She died.
33	LAURA: *(Furious. Draws back. She is unable to face this even*
34	*knowing it to be true.)* You know, you really are a horrible
35	little man.

1	NEELY: *(Completely unperturbed)* **Laura, your daughter was**
2	**not taken — like put in a foster home or sent to live with**
3	**her father. She died. She developed pneumonia and**
4	**couldn't fight it through. You and Brady were living in**
5	**the trailer at the time.**
6	LAURA: *(High)* Neely, I cannot talk about that tonight.
7	NEELY: What night would be suitable?
8	LAURA: *(Sobs)* Oh, you — *(Relaxes some.)* Oh, wouldn't you
9	think the pain would let up by now? I mean it. Four years
10	later. Four years and forty-four cases of scotch later.
11	NEELY: No, I wouldn't think it helped.
12	LAURA: *(Goes right on.)* By now, I'd — get it out of my head. I
13	never hurt anyone. Not that I know of. I was a nice girl.
14	My parents always said they never had a moment's worry
15	with me.
16	NEELY: You really want it out of your head?
17	LAURA: Yes. No. I ran back into the hospital that day and
18	started screaming.
19	NEELY: The nurses quieted you down but couldn't get you
20	to go home.
21	LAURA: *(High)* You don't know. She tried so hard to live.
22	Momma! Momma! Oh, my God. She was only four years
23	old, and I prayed. I prayed so hard and I promised —
24	anything — anything — *(Shakes her head.)* It was no use.
25	No bargains were to be made. *(There is a long silence.*
26	*NEELY hugs LAURA and she stays in his arms. They rock back*
27	*and forth a little. Finally she speaks.)* I didn't offer you any
28	coffee. What a marvelous hostess.
29	NEELY: No, you didn't.
30	LAURA: All recovered drunks want coffee. Step number one.
31	NEELY: I was in charge of making it for three months at our
32	AA meetings. Remember?
33	LAURA: Oh, Neely, do you think I'll ever hear from Brady
34	again?
35	NEELY: Do you want to?

1	LAURA: *(Ruefully)* Well, you don't get a husband every day of
2	the week.
3	NEELY: You didn't answer my question.
4	LAURA: I guess I do. I failed him so many times . . . .
5	NEELY: Like hell you did.
6	LAURA: I did. I shouldn't have panicked that night and
7	screamed at him — it was his fault — the trailer was
8	always cold —
9	NEELY: You were upset.
10	LAURA: He was her daddy . . . Then I started punishing the
11	scotch — and still the screaming didn't stop.
12	NEELY: It will. Everything fades.
13	LAURA: Oh, what a life I made for myself.
14	NEELY: Stop that.
15	LAURA: No. I hate it.
16	NEELY: You're working steady. Your boss at the warehouse
17	is nice.
18	LAURA: My baby gone. Drunk for a year. Then off the alcohol
19	and on to the pills. Running from doctor to doctor for
20	new prescriptions. You'd be surprised how easy some of
21	those doctors are.
22	NEELY: OK, Mrs. Corrigan, you've downed yourself enough
23	now.
24	LAURA: *(Nods)* Yes. Enough.
25	NEELY: How about taking a little credit.
26	LAURA: *(Laughs bitterly.)* First place in the dumb dodo
27	division?
28	NEELY: You've been straight two years.
29	LAURA: Me and half a million others.
30	NEELY: Off pills for two years.
31	LAURA: No argument.
32	NEELY: You went through eight days of being detoxed.
33	Twenty-eight days at Clear Springs Rehabilitation
34	Center. You've started on the twelve steps AA pushes for
35	all its members.

1	LAURA:	And all that added together doesn't spell "mother,"
2		Mr. Shambach.
3	NEELY:	Maybe not. It spells one heck of a gal, though.
4	LAURA:	You've been dry for four years.
5	NEELY:	Look, hon, I didn't wait around for an accident to get
6		going. I was stealing my old man's sippin' whiskey when
7		I was ten. At fifteen, I was trying to get sober. I'm nineteen
8		now. Now, *that* was a life.
9	LAURA:	Oh, Neely, why us?
10	NEELY:	Why anybody, hon? You take a drink. Then you take
11		two. Then you take twenty-two. It's something called an
12		addictive predilection. The lucky ones and the unlucky
13		ones are both trying to find out why.
14	LAURA:	I wish I'd been one of the lucky ones, Neely.
15	NEELY:	And miss what you've learned?
16	LAURA:	What life looks like from the gutter?
17	NEELY:	Isn't any experience useful?
18	LAURA:	There's a lot of good books out on that subject. But
19		there's one thing that happened — I found you at that
20		first AA meeting. *(Remembers)* "My name is Laura, and I'm
21		a drunk."
22	NEELY:	You didn't need me. You'd have made it, no matter
23		who you tied up with as a sponsor. *(She rests in his arms.*
24		*The telephone rings. He releases her and she answers.)*
25	LAURA:	Hello . . . Oh, my heavens! *(She holds the phone away*
26		*from her.)*
27	NEELY:	Who is it?
28	LAURA:	It's . . . I don't believe it . . . *(Back to phone)* Brady? Is
29		that you, Brady? It's me. Laura . . . Oh, honey, are you
30		coming home? . . . Of course I'm sober. I'm the most sober
31		wife you've ever seen . . . I'd love to see you, honey . . . Oh,
32		Brady, I'm going to cry . . . *(Blackout)*
33		
34		
35		

Getting Started

Cast of Characters

KELLY DREISBACH

21, feisty, pretty. Isn't afraid to talk up, violent about equal rights for women. Pennsylvania Dutch, but not tradition-minded.

JOSHUA DREISBACH

Kelly's brother, about 23. Just a shade cocksure, used to making decisions. More traditionally Pennsylvania Dutch.

MIKE PEACHY

24, good-looking, a nice guy; is he or isn't he a con-man? (Actually, he's not.)

NOTE

The Pennsylvania Dutch accent and expressions used by the character, JOSHUA, should not be played broadly. Substituting the letter "V" for "W" and vice versa is pretty standard among the Plain People. Ending sentences using the words, "still," "yet," "already," and "once," are also traditional.

1   *AT RISE:* The kitchen at JOSHUA DREISBACH's home near
2   Lancaster, Pennsylvania. JOSHUA is of Pennsylvania Dutch
3   descent and the home furnishings reflect this. He is dressed in
4   jeans, work shirt, and the traditional broad-brimmed hat.
5   KELLY, his sister, is with him, but she is "Gay Dutch," those
6   who have broken with tradition in dress and actions. At the
7   moment, KELLY looks dejected.
8
9   JOSHUA: Ach, Kelly. Such a face you make still.
10 KELLY: Joshua, nothing's going to work out for my trip.
11 JOSHUA: Kelly, it will. I —
12 KELLY: My roommate at Lawson — you've heard me talk
13   about Marion Kushner —
14 JOSHUA: Marion. Yes.
15 KELLY: She teaches political science — matter of fact, my
16   psychology classes meet at the same time as hers — we're
17   even in the same building — Hunt Hall — well, she
18   promised to drive down with me, then backed out at the
19   last minute.
20 JOSHUA: People get busy, Kelly. That's why I decided —
21 KELLY: *(Not listening)* Then two women in the astronomy lab
22   told me — well, right after we heard Aunt Ellie was
23   critically ill — oh, yes, they wanted to see Florida. Oh,
24   yes, since we had a long semester break, they'd love to
25   go with me and share the driving chore —
26 JOSHUA: Sister, could I cut in once right here?
27 KELLY: Then you disappointed me. "If you can't get anyone,
28   I'll go with you," you said. There should be someone from
29   our family at the reading of Aunt Ellie's will in Florida.
30   I don't expect anything, really, but it's the respect.
31 JOSHUA: Kelly, listen such a minute now. I never promised
32   I'd —
33 KELLY: Yes, you did. We were sitting right here in your
34   kitchen. Like we are now. I said I'd bought a new red
35   Jaguar convertible —

1   JOSHUA: So expensive yet, Sister. But a $\underline{w}$ery nice car.
2   KELLY: I know. On an assistant professor's salary at a small
3   college. Sheer madness. And totally out of keeping with
4   my Pennsylvania Dutch upbringing, but —
5   JOSHUA: I said I'd go if I could get some vacation time. But
6   you know the State Farm Show comes up in Harrisburg
7   the beginning of January. We have four cows ready to
8   deliver soon. And the chores around the farm — ach,
9   Kelly, such a time still!
10 KELLY: It's OK. Everyone else poops out on me. Why shouldn't
11   my only brother?
12 JOSHUA: You can't take an airplane already?
13 KELLY: I don't want to fly. Or go by bus. Or train. I wouldn't
14   have bought the car otherwise.
15 JOSHUA: $\underline{V}$ell, Kelly, just for once, I hired a driver to help you
16   out.
17 KELLY: *(Only half hears.)* **The automobile club's been marvelous**
18   **about giving me directions and maps. I'll get lost —**
19   **naturally, but —** *(Double take)* **You did what?**
20 JOSHUA: Not to get upset, Sister.
21 KELLY: Joshua, I'm already upset.
22 JOSHUA: It's the Travel Anywhere Driver Service in Lancaster
23   yet. It's a $\underline{w}$ery reliable firm. The drivers are bonded. They
24   act like chauffeurs once. Then they fly back from wherever
25   they take you.
26 KELLY: Joshua, you can't do that!
27 JOSHUA: $\underline{V}$y not?
28 KELLY: I'd be uncomfortable — it's OK to go with a woman
29   — but traveling alone with a man —
30 JOSHUA: Kelly, you're not getting hitched-up married. This
31   is a business arrangement.
32 KELLY: Then you go if it's so darned businessy.
33 JOSHUA: As for taking your own part, Sister, remember,
34   you beat up George Meachem in fourth grade.
35 KELLY: *(Secretly pleased)* **Oh, I did not. He tripped and fell.**

1   JOSHUA: Ach, never. You punched his lights out. Like they
2   say on tele<u>w</u>ision. Then his father —
3   KELLY: It was his mother.
4   JOSHUA: — Came over to make a law case because you'd
5   knocked out his two front teeth.
6   KELLY: Oh, you're making me sound horrible.
7   JOSHUA: Such black eyes you gave him.
8   KELLY: Joshua! Let's talk about this driver. Now, what's the
9   man's name already?
10   JOSHUA: His name?
11   KELLY: Yes, his name.
12   JOSHUA: <u>V</u>ell, that's funny.
13   KELLY: You don't know. You have that same dumb look on
14   your face you had in seventh grade algebra class when
15   Miss Burrows called on you.
16   JOSHUA: I didn't have algebra in seventh grade. And to
17   answer your question, Miss Fresh-As-Paint, it's not
18   re<u>w</u>ealed to the customers. The lady said it was according
19   to the driver board. They take turns. Like the grocery
20   store meat counter where you take a number still.
21   KELLY: Oh, Joshua, I wish you hadn't.
22   JOSHUA: Not?
23   KELLY: Not.
24   JOSHUA: Kelly, Poppa used to say women are too emotional
25   to make important decisions.
26   KELLY: Save me from tradition! That was two hundred years
27   ago, Joshua.
28   JOSHUA: My wife, Abigail, always respects my judgment.
29   KELLY: Well, that's all very beautiful and sweet, and that's
30   your business, yours and Abigail's. But I'm considered
31   "Gay Dutch," not "Traditional Dutch," Josh. So I'll thank
32   you to stay out of my affairs in the future. OK?
33   JOSHUA: Ach, it's your life, little sister. *(The roar of a motor,*
34   *then tires squealing is heard off. JOSHUA runs to the window.*
35   *KELLY reacts.)*

1	KELLY:	Great heavens, what's that?
2	JOSHUA:	Someone on a motorcycle still.
3	KELLY:	Mister "X"?
4	JOSHUA:	I don't know.
5	KELLY:	When I called you last night, and you said everything
6		was arranged and all squared away, I should have known.
7		*(Doorbell)*
8	JOSHUA:	I'll let him in.
9	KELLY:	No, I'll answer it.
10	JOSHUA:	Maybe it would look better if I —
11	KELLY:	Oh, Joshie, go sit on a — a —
12	JOSHUA:	Such a tack?
13	KELLY:	No — a load of corncobs. *(KELLY opens door. Standing*
14		*there is MIKE PEACHY, wearing a blue blazer with the travel*
15		*company's logo on it.)* **Well, hello.**
16	MIKE:	Miss Dreisbach? Kelly Dreisbach?
17	KELLY:	Yes.
18	MIKE:	I'm Mike Peachy. Your driver from the travel agency.
19	KELLY:	Come in. This is my brother, Joshua. He's really the
20		one who called you.
21	MIKE:	But you're the one making the trip?
22	KELLY:	So far. *(MIKE looks blank.)* **Just kidding.**
23	MIKE:	If that's your car out front, the red Jaguar —
24	KELLY:	It is.
25	MIKE:	Super-looking job.
26	JOSHUA:	Mr. Peachy, my sister and I have been talking, and
27		just to settle things —
28	MIKE:	Call me Mike.
29	JOSHUA:	We'd like to see your identification — a proof who
30		you are already.
31	KELLY:	*(Thinking aloud)* **Peachy. Peachy. Sounds** as
32		Pennsylvania Dutch as Dreisbach.
33	MIKE:	It is. My parents live in Belleville.
34	KELLY:	That's only twenty miles away.
35	MIKE:	Well, yeah, I guess so. Actually, I only do this driving

1   part-time.

2   KELLY: Oh?

3   MIKE: Well, I — I have a regular job. With the state. In
4   Harrisburg.

5   JOSHUA: Ach.

6   MIKE: Not to brag or anything, I'm a good driver. Never had
7   an accident. *(Looks around.)* **Knock on wood.** *(He does.)*

8   JOSHUA: Vell, we're vaiting yet. For the identification.

9   MIKE: *(Digs out his wallet.)* No problem. Here's my driver's
10   license. It's a pretty grungy picture, but it's me.

11 JOSHUA: No. Such proof is not right.

12 MIKE: I — ah — well, as a matter of fact, I don't have anything
13   from the company.

14 JOSHUA: Not none?

15 KELLY: Josh, give the man a chance.

16 JOSHUA: Sister, once you should — hold your tongue still,
17   please.

18 KELLY: Joshua, take it easy.

19 JOSHUA: Now, I'm older than you, Sister.

20 KELLY: Joshua, one of these days I'm going to trade you in
21   for a better model.

22 JOSHUA: Yah, after once I see this man's identification.

23 KELLY: Oh, for heaven's sake, Mike. Show him some
24   identification.

25 MIKE: *(Stuttering)* Well — as a matter of fact — the point is —
26   I'm not sure I have anything from the company.

27 JOSHUA: Chust an identification will do.

28 MIKE: I know that.

29 JOSHUA: And you don't have some?

30 MIKE: No.

31 JOSHUA: Nothing like?

32 MIKE: Nothing that would satisfy you.

33 JOSHUA: Vell, I'll tell you, Mike. Ve don't like this way of
34   doing sings. Ach, it's too fishy for half.

35 MIKE: I can explain it.

1	JOSHUA: Kelly, I sink we have to call the company, not? This
2	is not proper. Wearing the company coat and all.
3	MIKE: I assure you, I'm doing nothing wrong.
4	JOSHUA: Then it's OK with you if we check?
5	KELLY: Maybe you have to check, Josh. I'm not all that
6	concerned.
7	JOSHUA: If you vould gif me the telephone number on that
8	card I gave you already, Kelly.
9	KELLY: Let's see. 291-6 —
10	MIKE: Ah — *(KELLY and JOSHUA look up.)* Save yourself the
11	trouble. There's no use your calling the company.
12	JOSHUA: Say not?
13	MIKE: I — I don't work for the company.
14	JOSHUA: Ach!
15	KELLY: But what's going on? Why pretend you do?
16	MIKE: They won't know who I am. *(There is a long silence.)*
17	JOSHUA: So! So who are you then?
18	MIKE: Mike Peachy. Just as I told you. And my folks do live in
19	Belleville. Only the truth is — maybe I should have told
20	you this from the beginning . . . .
21	JOSHUA: Yeah, maybe.
22	MIKE: It's my roommate, Paul Hufnagle, who works for them.
23	JOSHUA: Another lie?
24	MIKE: No, I'm not lying. I never do. He's sick. The flu. He's
25	had a lot of time off lately. He really has. Appendicitis
26	operation eight weeks ago. Then he broke his left ankle
27	three weeks later playing in a YMCA basketball game.
28	He was afraid they'd can him if he took off any more
29	time, so I told him I'd take the job. This is his blazer I'm
30	wearing. There's really nothing wrong with it, I assure
31	you, only — I was trying to do my roommate a favor. What
32	difference does it make which one of us does the driving?
33	JOSHUA: It von't do. No, sir. Such a fish story in our wery
34	kitchen. I'd adwise you to get off our property before I
35	call the police.

1　　MIKE:　I know it looks funny, but —

2　　JOSHUA:　Now, scat, already. Shoo! *(MIKE starts out.)*

3　　KELLY:　Mike, wait a minute.

4　　JOSHUA:　Kelly, keep out of this still.

5　　KELLY:　No. You keep out of it. *(JOSHUA and KELLY stand*

6　　　　*there and glare at each other. This isn't about MIKE's identity.*

7　　　　*This is about sibling rivalry and who's in charge.)*

8　　JOSHUA:　I told you —

9　　KELLY:　Mike, I want to hear the rest of your story even if my

10　　　　brother doesn't.

11　　JOSHUA:　Kelly, I cannot allow — you're making a mistake.

12　　KELLY:　Maybe. I've made dozens of them. But I'm the one

13　　　　who's making this trip. Whose car is being used. Whose

14　　　　safety is involved. So — keep those ideas in front of you,

15　　　　Joshua.

16　　JOSHUA:　Not vhere my only sister is —

17　　KELLY:　And I'll tell you something else I feel, Joshua. I'm

18　　　　making the decisions here.

19　　JOSHUA:　Kelly, I von't allow it. I'm not standing to such a

20　　　　side and letting you —

21　　KELLY:　This time, I'm telling you.

22　　JOSHUA:　Kelly. Now, hear me out . . . *(JOSHUA and KELLY*

23　　　　*stare at each other. MIKE is motionless as we go to black.)*

24

25

26

27

28

29

30

31

32

33

34

35

Sudden Encounter

Cast of Characters

PHYLLIS HARPER

Age 30, rather severely dressed. A business woman who has won her way to the top despite a nasty, unfair occurence in her earlier life. She is bitter, triumphant, and a little hard at first, but caution must be observed not to make her a caricature as she mellows considerably.

MRS. LANDIS

About 50, a woman who jumps to conclusions knowing only half the story; hard-working, not overly bright, a plodder.

GLENN HARPER

Phyllis' husband, 32, straight arrow; nice, tolerant, in love with Phyllis, considerate.

MISS CONCINNI

Intercom voice.

1   *AT RISE:* The personnel director's office of Franklin's,
2   Philadelphia's largest department store. It is nicely furnished.
3   Discovered is PHYLLIS HARPER. She should come off as firm
4   and responsive as much as vindictive.
5
6   PHYLLIS: *(Speaks into intercom.)* **Yes?**
7   INTERCOM VOICE: **Mrs. Melvin G. Landis is in the waiting**
8   **room, Mrs. Harper.**
9   PHYLLIS: **Thanks, Miss Concinni. Send her in.** *(Door opens.)*
10 INTERCOM VOICE: *(Off)* **You may go in now, Mrs. Landis.**
11 MRS. LANDIS: *(As she enters)* **Thank you.**
12 PHYLLIS: *(Into intercom)* **That'll be all, Miss Concinni. Please,**
13   **close the door.** *(Door is closed. MRS. LANDIS enters speaking.)*
14 MRS. LANDIS: *(Surprised)* **The section head said you wanted**
15   **to — why, it's Phyllis — Phyllis Harper.**
16 PHYLLIS: **Sit down, Mrs. Landis.**
17 MRS. LANDIS: **Well, I had no idea.**
18 PHYLLIS: **I'm sure you didn't.**
19 MRS. LANDIS: **When the woman at the employment office**
20   **told me I was wanted by the head of personnel of**
21   **Franklin's, the biggest department store in Philadelphia,**
22   **I never thought I'd —**
23 PHYLLIS: **Come face to face with me?**
24 MRS. LANDIS: **Now, *you* do the hiring.**
25 PHYLLIS: **Yes. Funny, isn't it?**
26 MRS. LANDIS: **I certainly hated to leave Harrisburg, Phyllis.**
27   **But things just went from bad to worse in my little dress**
28   **shop. So many shopping malls opened up on the outskirts**
29   **of the city. Free parking. Movies. Free entertainment.**
30   **What didn't they have? You should see our downtown.**
31   **It's like a ghost city with all the empty stores. I had no**
32   **choice. I closed up, and now I'm job hunting.**
33 PHYLLIS: **So now you're a Christmas extra.**
34 MRS. LANDIS: **Phyllis, I hope you still don't feel — well, still**
35   **don't feel that I —**

1   PHYLLIS: What's the matter, Mrs. Landis?

2   MRS. LANDIS: I did what I thought was right, Phyllis. I admit

3   I made a mistake when I accused you of stealing money

4   from my store when you worked for me. I admit I was

5   hasty in firing you too. But —

6   PHYLLIS: But you're sorry now, aren't you? You wouldn't

7   harm anyone intentionally, would you?

8   MRS. LANDIS: You're not going to hold it against me?

9   PHYLLIS: I've been checking over our lists. I find we've taken

10   on too many people — some of them will have to be let go.

11   MRS. LANDIS: Phyllis, I did a terrible thing. I know it. But

12   it's not fair to —

13   PHYLLIS: You talk of fairness to me! You dare. The girl you

14   threw out of your store. The one you branded a thief.

15   *(Furious)* Do you know what that's like?

16   MRS. LANDIS: It was in the paper — about Janie being the

17   guilty one — everyone knew —

18   PHYLLIS: What did they know? About the agony you put me

19   through? About your malicious tongue? About shutting

20   myself up in my room when I couldn't stand their staring

21   eyes any longer? About chasing me out of my hometown?

22   MRS. LANDIS: I didn't. I never meant to.

23   PHYLLIS: I can't ever go back. If I wanted to, I couldn't go

24   back. Do you know why, Mrs. Landis? *Because I'm not*

25   *nice.* I'm the girl they talked about.

26   MRS. LANDIS: Phyllis, I need the job. I have to —

27   PHYLLIS: That's what I told Miss Johnson. Remember her?

28   She ran a little candy store. I needed a job too then. But

29   you'd done your work too well. Nobody wanted me in

30   Harrisburg.

31   MRS. LANDIS: *(Wildly)* I'll get another job. This isn't the only

32   store in —

33   PHYLLIS: Not when I'm through with you, you won't. I'll

34   have you black-listed in every department store in

35   Philadelphia — if I have to telephone them myself. I'm

going to give you a chance to know what it's like, Mrs.
Landis. Now you can see how it feels to be hunted.
(Blackout)

(The Philadelphia apartment of PHYLLIS and GLENN HARPER. Early evening. GLENN is sitting. PHYLLIS is too stimulated to sit down.)

PHYLLIS: *(Exultantly)* **Oh, Glenn, if you could only have seen her face. I tell you it was worth it. Everything I'd gone through —**

GLENN: **Looked pretty sad, eh?**

PHYLLIS: **Sad? Her chin was down around her ankles. If she wasn't cursing the day she was born —**

GLENN: **I wonder what she'll do now?**

PHYLLIS: **What do I care what she does? Let her get a job scrubbing — that's about what she deserves.**

GLENN: **She isn't so young anymore, Phyl.**

PHYLLIS: **Well, for heaven's sake, stop feeling sorry for her.**

GLENN: **I can't help it.**

PHYLLIS: **Nobody felt sorry for me.**

GLENN: **I did. I think she did too when she realized —**

PHYLLIS: **Isn't that just like you?**

GLENN: **You know, I've never seen you exactly like this before.**

PHYLLIS: **I suppose you preferred me cringing — hiding in corners.**

GLENN: **No, but you came out and fought clean then.**

PHYLLIS: **What am I doing now? Punching under the belt?**

GLENN: **What do you think?**

PHYLLIS: **I think she got what she deserved.**

GLENN: **Then that's all there is to it. Well, what's for supper?**

PHYLLIS: **Don't you?**

GLENN: **Don't I what? If you want me to tell you I approve —**

PHYLLIS: **I am waiting.**

GLENN: **Well, I don't. I don't like it.**

PHYLLIS: **You're criticizing me?**

GLENN: **Because essentially I know you're above a cheap**

1   trick like that.

2 PHYLLIS: It wasn't a cheap trick. I tell you it wasn't. She had
3   it coming.

4 GLENN: All right!

5 PHYLLIS: *(Near tears)* She did! She had it coming. And I think
6   you're unfair — and mean and — *(Runs to door, opens it.*
7   *Starts to run out. His voice stops her.)*

8 GLENN: Phyl, come back here. Where are you going?

9 PHYLLIS: I'm going out. Where you don't need to look at me.
10   You don't like me the way I am, anyway! *(A long sob. She*
11   *disappears, slams door. Blackout.)*

12   *(The apartment again — much later. Clock strikes five. Key in*
13   *lock. Door opens, PHYLLIS enters. GLENN is sleeping on sofa.*
14   *He wakes the minute PHYLLIS enters.)*

15 GLENN: Phyl? Phyl, is that you?

16 PHYLLIS: *(Wearily)* Hello, Glenn.

17 GLENN: Where've you been? I've been calling all over town —

18 PHYLLIS: I'm so tired. I've been walking.

19 GLENN: Since seven? What on earth —

20 PHYLLIS: I stopped for coffee. I'll bet I had ten cups.

21 GLENN: Look at you. Look at your hair, Phyl. If you don't —

22 PHYLLIS: I was thinking too, Glenn. About what you said.

23 GLENN: Oh.

24 PHYLLIS: And you were right. I knew you were. All the time.

25 GLENN: Oh, Phyl.

26 PHYLLIS: That's why I ran away. Only you can't run away
27   from yourself. No matter how hard you try. *(Breaks)* Oh,
28   Glenn, I'm so ashamed. I have to find Mrs. Landis . . . find
29   her and make it right again. *(Blackout)*

30

31

32

33

34

35

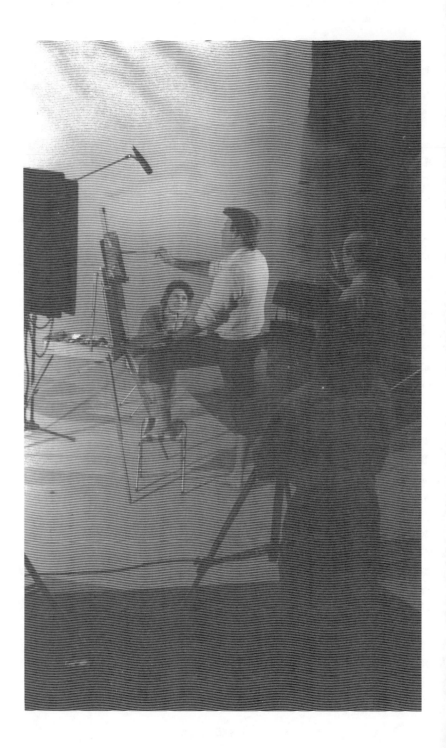

To See Ourselves

Cast of Characters

MELISSA THOMAS
Age 15-16, coltish, in love with love. A dreamer, yet with a stubborn streak.

FATHER
About 60, Melissa's father; highly protective of the girl.

MOTHER
Melissa's mother, also about 60. Feels just as protective of Melissa, but softer about it.

ERIC PETERS
Age 34, an artist and a romantic. Enjoys the attention of a young girl.

1   *AT RISE:*   Outdoors — water, woods, sky. ERIC PETERS is
2   painting. MELISSA THOMAS is sitting by, watching with
3   admiration and — love.
4
5   ERIC: Don't you ever get tired watching me paint, Melissa?
6   MELISSA: Oh, no, Eric.
7   ERIC: Well, you've a lot more patience than my wife, Lenora.
8   MELISSA: Is she — is she pretty?
9   ERIC: Lenora? I suppose so. In a sort of cameo-style.
10   MELISSA: I wish I looked like that!
11   ERIC: You have more than just that, Melissa. Your face has
12   good lines — and strength. A *beautiful* strength.
13   MELISSA: My face is — I know what I look like.
14   ERIC: Oh, come on now . . . you ought to have more confidence
15   in yourself. You have intelligence and a kind of inner
16   radiance that puts you head and shoulders above most
17   girls.
18   MELISSA: Don't try to be kind, please, Eric.
19   ERIC: No, I mean it. Do you think I'd have wanted to be with
20   you all this time if I didn't think you were different?
21   Better than the rest . . . .
22   MELISSA: Do you think that about me, Eric? Do you really?
23   ERIC: I think you're one of the most charming girls I've ever
24   known.
25   MELISSA: *(High)* Oh, Eric. Eric, I don't think I've ever been
26   so happy. Just meeting you on the beach like we did and
27   being with you makes me wish I never had to see anybody
28   else again. My parents or my friends . . . or — or anybody.
29   ERIC: *(Laughs)* You're a sweet child. But it's getting late.
30   Come on. We'd better get back to town. *(Blackout)*
31   *(Kitchen of the Thomas house. Tastefully done — soft lighting,*
32   *perhaps a reproduction of a Tiffany shade over the table.*
33   *MELISSA is dreamily putting dishes in the cupboard. FATHER*
34   *comes on holding a newspaper.)*
35   FATHER: Melissa, as soon as you've finished with those

1	dishes, Mother and I want to have a talk with you.
2	*(MOTHER follows FATHER into kitchen.)*
3	MELISSA: I'm done now, Poppa. What is it?
4	MOTHER: Now, Frank, remember.
5	FATHER: Let me handle this, Mother. And I'm coming
6	straight to the point. Who is this Eric Peters, Melissa?
7	MELISSA: *(Dreamily)* He's — well, he's a friend of mine.
8	FATHER: I gathered that much. What I want to know is, who
9	is he? Where'd he come from? What's he doing here?
10	MELISSA: He's an artist. He came to Pawling's Station to paint.
11	FATHER: And what does his painting have to do with you?
12	MELISSA: *(Realizing)* I don't know what you mean.
13	MOTHER: Now, Frank, you're not saying what we planned at
14	all.
15	MELISSA: What you planned to? What is all this?
16	FATHER: I'm through beating around the bush. People
17	are talking, Melissa. There's three thousand people in
18	Pawling's Station. Everyone knows all about everyone
19	else. By George, I won't have my daughter running
20	around with a married man.
21	MELISSA: Who told you that?
22	FATHER: Is it true?
23	MELISSA: Is what true? That Eric and I have talked together?
24	That we've gone picnicking?
25	FATHER: Without our permission.
26	MELISSA: Your permission! I haven't done anything that
27	needs your permission!
28	MOTHER: Melissa, please understand. We're only thinking
29	of you.
30	FATHER: I don't want to ever hear of your talking to that
31	man again. Understand, Melissa? *Let this be the end of it!*
32	*(He exits. As he goes, speaks to MOTHER.)* Come along, Mother.
33	MOTHER: *(Remains)* Darling, Poppa puts things so bluntly.
34	MELISSA: Don't apologize for him. He said what he wanted
35	to say.

1　MOTHER:　We're only thinking of your own good. Oh, Melissa,
2　　　I know you think it's impossible — looking at me now —
3　　　but I was your age once. Yes, and had your dreams, too.
4　MELISSA:　I don't want to discuss it.
5　MOTHER:　But, darling, we must discuss it.
6　MELISSA:　Times have changed since you were in high
7　　　school.
8　MOTHER:　They have indeed, but one thing that hasn't
9　　　changed is the reputation a girl gets when word gets
10　　　around she's seeing a married man on the sly.
11　MELISSA:　On the sly! How ridiculous. I've never done
12　　　anything on the sly in my life.
13　MOTHER:　And that's what makes it even worse — your being
14　　　so honest. Oh, Melissa, there were — fast girls in my day
15　　　too. They always sat together in The Sweet Shop — and
16　　　sat alone, I might add, poor devils.
17　MELISSA:　You don't understand a single solitary thing I feel,
18　　　Mother.
19　MOTHER:　*(Goes right on.)* So when the fellows came in, and we
20　　　all danced, it wasn't that crowd of girls who danced with
21　　　the fellows. Oh, they were over there laughing and
22　　　giggling up a storm, but it all sounded so — hollow
23　　　somehow. Not that the fellows didn't meet them at some
24　　　time, I guess. But they certainly didn't meet them or
25　　　recognize them in The Sweet Shop. That's why Daddy
26　　　and I don't want —
27　MELISSA:　Mamma, I love Eric.
28　MOTHER:　You — *(Gasps)* What are you saying?
29　MELISSA:　He loves me too. He told me. Oh, how I've wanted
30　　　to tell you. To share it with someone. For the first time
31　　　in my life, I was proud. He says he likes me better than
32　　　any other girl he's ever known.
33　MOTHER:　And you believed that? From a married man?
34　MELISSA:　Believed it. *(She laughs.)* You don't know. I think
35　　　I'd have died for him then.

1	MOTHER:	Melissa, you mustn't say that.
2	MELISSA:	He wants to divorce his wife and marry me. I know
3		he does.
4	MOTHER:	Divorce. Marrying a man twice your age! With a
5		wife and children. Melissa, it simply can't be.
6	MELISSA:	But it is. And I'm not listening to you, Mamma.
7		For the first time in my life, I'm not listening to you.
8	MOTHER:	Melissa, I — no, don't force me to do it.
9	MELISSA:	To do what? You can't do anything.
10	MOTHER:	I received a letter this morning. One that Mr.
11		Peters wrote — your Eric — to his wife. She sent it back
12		to me with a note of her own.
13	MELISSA:	It's not true. Eric wouldn't do that.
14	MOTHER:	This time you'll have to listen. *(Pulls letter from*
15		*apron, reads.)* "I've met the oddest girl here, Lenora. One
16		that I'd almost like you to know, except that if the two
17		of you ever came face to face, I think she'd scratch your
18		eyes out. You see, she's fallen in love with me. All of which
19		was not in the script at all." Shall I go on?
20	MELISSA:	Go on —
21	MOTHER:	"Her name is Melissa Thomas, and she's just
22		sixteen. Maybe only fifteen. Remember when you were
23		that age, Lenora? You were so lovely. But, Melissa — well,
24		she's certainly no beauty — although her plain little face
25		is really very interesting. Almost exciting in a way.
26		Unfortunately, I don't believe anyone but me has ever
27		noticed it. I wonder if anyone ever will."
28	MELISSA:	Oh — Mother — Mother — how could he?
29	MOTHER:	You'd better hear the rest. "She's so shy and
30		painfully scared that I felt I had to do something for her.
31		Apparently she's been waiting a long time for a man to
32		be interested in her because we've since swept along in
33		the most whirlwind of romances. And if I can avoid
34		hurting her too deeply, it should do her a world of good.
35		I'm honestly hoping it will. No one — no matter who she is

1 — should be denied completely the thrill of being
2 interesting and important to someone. Since I'll only be
3 here another month or so, she can always remember
4 me —"
5 MELISSA: *(Hysterically crying)* **Stop it, Mamma! Stop it!**
6 *(Blackout)*

A Case of Mistaken Identity

Cast of Characters

TINA McFELLOWS
Aunt Tina is 55, rich, a gadabout, cute, appealing and mischievous. She loves young men and they return her affection. She is impulsive, generous and nearsighted. Also, too vain to wear glasses.

MAGGIE BLAKE
Tina's niece is 24, pretty, and down to earth; a steadying influence for Tina.

ARTHUR HODGES
Age 30, he is kind of a comfortable doormat. He is a staid conservative lawyer, really a nice looking guy who feels the need to "help."

TED COLLIER
Everything comes easily to Ted, 30. Handsome, with a sparkling sense of humor.

1   *AT RISE:*   The plush living room of TINA McFELLOWS. She is
2   standing at an open door waving goodbye. MAGGIE is with her.
3

4   TINA: *(Calling)* **Goodbye. Goodbye, Sergeant Daniels.**
5   **Remember, the next time you're in Newport, I want you**
6   **for dinner again.** *(Turns to MAGGIE.)* **Oh, wasn't he just**
7   **the sweetest Marine you've ever seen, Maggie?**
8   MAGGIE: **He was very nice, Aunt Tina, but I'd hardly call a**
9   **six-foot-four bruiser like that** *sweet.*
10   TINA: **You know, all the time we were watching that mystery**
11   **play on television, when the lights were low, he was**
12   **holding my hand.** *(Sighs)* **I just love protective Marines.**
13   MAGGIE: *(Chiding)* **Oh, Aunt Tina.** *(Change)* **Come along, we'd**
14   **better go inside and see how Arthur's making out with**
15   **those dishes.**
16   TINA: **In a minute. It was so romantic the way we met at the**
17   **drugstore. I mean, Sergeant Daniels and I. He was asking**
18   **for razor blades and I was asking for toothpaste — and**
19   **then I stepped on his foot. That's what started it all off,**
20   **really.**
21   MAGGIE: **Well, if you'd only wear your glasses, Tina, you**
22   **wouldn't be stepping on peoples' feet.**
23   TINA: **But then we wouldn't have met. Anyway, I don't really**
24   **need glasses. Those contacts hurt, and the other ones**
25   **make my nose look funny.**
26   MAGGIE: **Now, that's not so. My glasses don't make my nose**
27   **look funny.**
28   TINA: *(Thoughtfully)* **You know what, Maggie? I've decided**
29   **something.**
30   MAGGIE: **What now?**
31   TINA: **I like the Marines best of all — that lovely green**
32   **uniform. I'm going to bring more of them home — if I can**
33   **find them.**
34   MAGGIE: **Now, Aunt Tina, remember your promise.**
35   TINA: **Well, that's ridiculous. If a man's in a uniform, he's**

1	perfectly safe. It's my patriotic duty to be cordial to
2	servicemen, and when I see a lonely one, I'm going to
3	bring him home. I think I should invite two a week for
4	dinner — at least.
5	MAGGIE: But, Tina, Arthur says —
6	TINA: Arthur. Arthur. Arthur. Just because you're engaged
7	to Arthur doesn't say I can't have a — a bit of a fling. I'm
8	only thirty-eight, you know.
9	MAGGIE: You're what?
10	TINA: The girl that does my hair over at Cindy's says any
11	woman who's fifty-five nowadays is really only thirty-
12	eight because of — well, I forget the exact reason, but I
13	think it's their face cream. That peels off seventeen years.
14	*(Door opens and ARTHUR enters carrying a dishtowel and*
15	*wearing a kind of bartender's apron.)*
16	ARTHUR: *(Coming on)* Oh, Maggie, where do the soup plates
17	go?
18	MAGGIE: Oh, Arthur, you don't need to put them away. It's
19	enough that you pitched in and did all the washing.
20	ARTHUR: Well, I don't like leaving a disorderly kitchen.
21	Everything in its place.
22	TINA: If it's the Spode china, Arthur, that goes in the cupboard
23	— or is it the pantry? *(Vaguely)* Well, you know —
24	ARTHUR: And I noticed, Aunt Tina, that hulking Marine
25	burned a hole in your tablecloth. The Irish linen one.
26	TINA: Oh, did he? Well, give it to the rummage.
27	MAGGIE: We'll do no such thing. We can make napkins out of
28	that tablecloth if it's ruined. Honestly, Aunt Tina, the
29	way you throw money around, you'd think it grew on
30	trees.
31	ARTHUR: Margaret's right. You're running way over the
32	budget that I set up for you.
33	TINA: Arthur, for heaven's sake. I have five million dollars,
34	and you expect me to run this house on fifty dollars a
35	week.

1   ARTHUR: It's for your own good. A lawyer can see the value
2   of strict budgeting.
3   TINA: Now, don't bore me with figures, Arthur. It's too late,
4   and I don't understand them anyway. Besides, I'll have
5   all that on my hands next week.
6   MAGGIE: Goodness, I forgot. You're going to Washington
7   tomorrow. Are you all packed?
8   ARTHUR: And remember what I told you about those
9   Washington investments, Aunt Tina. In my opinion —
10   TINA: Oh, dear, I'm not at all packed yet. I'd better go up and
11   do that now. You send Arthur home and then come and
12   help me, Maggie.
13   MAGGIE: All right, darling.
14   TINA: *(Going off)* Good night, Arthur. You were very sweet to
15   do the dinner dishes. Especially since we couldn't get
16   Isabelle.
17   ARTHUR: You're welcome. You know that. Good night, Aunt
18   Tina.
19   MAGGIE: What's the matter, Arthur? Why are you looking
20   like that?
21   ARTHUR: Those men she keeps bringing home. It could be
22   dangerous. I don't like it, Margaret. Did you see the way
23   she looked at that Marine tonight?
24   MAGGIE: Oh, he was a baby. Nineteen years old.
25   ARTHUR: Still, a woman like Tina who's already had two
26   husbands — both of them fortune hunters, by the way —
27   well, who knows what can happen when we least expect
28   it.
29   MAGGIE: Oh, I don't think we need worry about Sergeant
30   Daniels. She'd hardly have her eye on him.
31   ARTHUR: After we're married, Margaret, between us, we're
32   going to have some changing to do as far as Aunt Tina's
33   romantic impulses are concerned. We have to get her
34   settled — make her recognize her age.
35   MAGGIE: Well, you know best, Arthur.

1	ARTHUR: I wish you were going to Washington with her.
2	I'll worry every minute of the time while she's gone.
3	MAGGIE: She'll only be there for five days.
4	ARTHUR: Well, I wish the trip were over. And she were
5	safely back in Newport. I'd feel a lot more comfortable.
6	Yes, I would. *(Blackout)*
7	*(Five days later. A railroad station platform. A few benches and*
8	*a sign reading "Newport, Rhode Island." Some extras could be*
9	*sitting on the benches, reading, etc.)*
10	MAGGIE: Arthur, why don't you sit down. The train'll be here.
11	ARTHUR: I'm sure of that, Margaret. The point is, *when* will
12	it be here?
13	MAGGIE: Well, the ticket agent told me that none of the
14	trains from Washington are running on schedule. He said
15	that —
16	ARTHUR: You realize we've wasted an hour and a half in
17	this station already waiting for Aunt Tina to come in. An
18	hour and a half that I could have used preparing my
19	briefs.
20	MAGGIE: I'm just as put out as you are, but if there's a train
21	running late, that's the one Aunt Tina'll be on.
22	ARTHUR: I hope everything's gone all right for her. If she'd
23	only let me handle her business. Tina's the type of woman
24	who should be home — knitting or something.
25	MAGGIE: Better not tell her that. She thinks I'm old-fashioned
26	for spending all that time on my needle-pointing.
27	ARTHUR: You're not old-fashioned, my dear. You're sensible,
28	steady and — and reliable. The highest qualities a woman
29	can have.
30	MAGGIE: Well, I try to be, Arthur. I suppose I'm even more
31	since I've lived with Tina so many years. Someone in the
32	house had to be efficient.
33	ARTHUR: You're very sweet, Margaret. And I think we're
34	admirably suited for each other. Not that ours is one of
35	those burning loves — the kind you read about — but I

1   like to feel that the two of us are like a quiet pond, gently
2   flowing over mossy earth.
3 MAGGIE: Well, Arthur, aren't you poetic for a lawyer. And
4   the city's most successful lawyer, too.
5 ARTHUR: *(Modestly)* Well, I suppose that's a moot question —
6   whether I'm *the* most successful or not.
7 MAGGIE: Oh, you are, Arthur. It's one of the things that
8   attracted me to you in the first place.
9 ARTHUR: It is?
10 MAGGIE: Oh, yes. Because I was sure you weren't interested
11   in the fact that I'll inherit all of Tina's money someday.
12 ARTHUR: Well, naturally. Not that we won't be more qualified
13   to handle it when you do get it.
14 MAGGIE: Right now, I'd settle for Tina's getting to this
15   station.
16 ARTHUR: Oh, dear. That train's an hour and forty minutes
17   late now. I don't like these upsets in my routine.
18 MAGGIE: Poor Tina. I'll bet she's worried sick about this
19   delay. I wonder what she's doing. *(Blackout)*
20   *(Fragment of a pullman seat on a moving train. TINA is calling.)*
21 TINA: Oh, young man. You in the blue uniform. Come here.
22 TED: Were you calling me, Ma'am?
23 TINA: Yes. Can you tell me when we'll be in Newport?
24 TED: In a couple of minutes, I believe.
25 TINA: Young man, I've been watching you.
26 TED: Why? Is something wrong?
27 TINA: Well, there certainly must be when a man in uniform
28   has to stand this entire trip. I think it's an outrage.
29 TED: Oh, but I'm used to it.
30 TINA: Nonsense. You sit over there — across from me where
31   we can look at each other.
32 TED: But, I —
33 TINA: Now, that man who was there won't be back. He went
34   to the diner.
35 TED: Well, I guess it'll be all right. It's only a mile or so yet.

1 TINA: Oh, it has been a long trip, hasn't it? But if I'd have
2   called you over sooner, I'll bet it would have just run by.
3   *(Light laugh)* Yes, it would.
4 TED: Well, thank you.
5 TINA: My, I love to see those blue uniforms. They're my
6   favorite. And yours looks so nice on you.
7 TED: Not much of a fit, I'm afraid.
8 TINA: Oh, no. Now you take the Marines for example. That
9   awful green uniform. They never seem to be quite right.
10 TED: Well, you couldn't say that about the outfit you have on.
11   That's a smart looking suit.
12 TINA: Do you think the hat's too ridiculous? I mean, all these
13   feathers — for a woman of my age.
14 TED: You have the kind of face that would set off any hat.
15 TINA: Now, you don't have to say that — not if you don't
16   mean it — but I hope you do.
17 TED: Of course I mean it.
18 TINA: Well, anyway, it's still nice. Look here, are you going
19   to Newport?
20 TED: Oh, yes. It's a large naval base.
21 TINA: I don't remember your face. Of course, I can't see you
22   too well — *(Covers up)* I mean, the car's so smokey — have
23   you always been there?
24 TED: No, but I expect to be for a couple of months.
25 TINA: Going to be stationed there?
26 TED: Well, I'm going to work out of Newport.
27 TINA: Now, I won't ask any more questions. I know certain
28   things are military secrets.
29 TED: *(Laughs)* Oh, I guess it isn't a military secret.
30 TINA: Tell me, who do you know in Newport? Who are your
31   friends?
32 TED: Oh, I don't know anyone. I'm from Chicago. But I'll get
33   to know people after I've been there for a while — I hope.
34 TINA: All alone in Newport — and on your first night too.
35   You know what?

1 TED: No, but I'll listen.
2 TINA: The time has come for introductions. I'm Mrs.
3   McFellows. Tina McFellows.
4 TED: How do you do, Mrs. McFellows. I'm Ted Collier.
5 TINA: Ted Collier. *(Cutely)* How are you? And how would you
6   like to have dinner with me tonight?
7 TED: Have dinner with you?
8 TINA: Now, I haven't shocked you, have I? It'll be a good
9   dinner. My niece, Maggie, lives with me. She's a very nice
10   girl. And then, her stuffy fiancé'll be there too, I suppose.
11   That would just make four of us.
12 TED: Two couples as a matter of fact.
13 TINA: Well, Ted, how gallant. Now I simply won't take no for
14   an answer.
15 TED: But maybe your niece wouldn't like it. Or the "stuffy
16   fiancé."
17 TINA: Well, it's my house. And Arthur — he's the stuffy one —
18   just criticizes all the time anyway. Please say you'll come.
19 TED: All right, Mrs. McFellows. Thanks. I'll be glad to.
20 TINA: Good.
21 TED: *(Standing)* Oh, we're coming into the station now.
22 TINA: I wonder if you'd help me with my bags, Ted.
23 TED: Sure thing. Where are they?
24 TINA: *(Pointing)* Why, they're — they're up there. They are,
25   aren't they? *(She peers.)*
26 TED: *(Grabs bags above seat.)* Yeah. Is this all you have?
27 TINA: Yes. Can you manage both of them?
28 TED: *(Train stops. We hear steam escaping, whistles.)* Yeah, I have
29   them. Come on, let's go out this way.
30 TINA: Which way?
31 TED: Right straight ahead.
32 TINA: Oh, yes, of course. I didn't see it at first. Now, we must
33   look for Margaret. She said she and Arthur would meet
34   me. *(Blackout.)*
35   *(TINA and TED come on the railroad platform set, TED carrying*

1   *TINA's luggage.)*

2   **TED:** Here now. Don't stumble on the platform. Take my arm.

3   *(She does.)* **Do you see your niece?**

4   **TINA:** No. Maybe I'd better put on my —

5   **MAGGIE:** *(Calling off. Comes on with ARTHUR.)* **Tina. Aunt**

6   **Tina. Here we are.**

7   **ARTHUR:** Hello, Mrs. McFellows. Hello. *(The women embrace.)*

8   **TINA:** Maggie, darling.

9   **MAGGIE:** Hello, Tina. How do you feel? Did you have a good

10   trip?

11   **TINA:** Of course, child. I always have a good trip.

12   **MAGGIE:** Arthur has his car parked over there.

13   **ARTHUR:** Can't let you walk, Aunt Tina.

14   **TINA:** Now stop making me feel old. I'll bet I'm a better walker

15   than you. Oh, I almost forgot. Ted, where are you?

16   **TED:** Right in back of you, Mrs. McFellows.

17   **TINA:** Maggie, this is Ted Collier. This is my niece, Miss

18   Blake. And that's Arthur Hodges.

19   **TED:** Hello, Miss Blake. Mr. Hodges.

20   **ARTHUR:** How do you do?

21   **MAGGIE:** Hello, Mr. Collier. Oh, you've got Tina's bags. Well,

22   thanks a lot. We'll take them now.

23   **TINA:** Oh, no. Ted's coming home for dinner with us.

24   **MAGGIE:** He's what?

25   **TINA:** Yes, we haven't had any servicemen for dinner in a

26   long time, Maggie. And it's our patriotic duty to be

27   sociable to the armed forces, you know. *(TED, MAGGIE,*

28   *and ARTHUR all speak at once.)*

29   **TED:** But I'm not —

30   **MAGGIE:** But he isn't —

31   **ARTHUR:** Why, he's not —

32   **TINA:** Now. Now. Not all at once.

33   **MAGGIE:** But, Tina, Mr. Collier's not in the armed forces.

34   **TINA:** What do you mean?

35   **TED:** Why, Mrs. McFellows, you could see that I'm —

1   MAGGIE: Wait a minute. You don't have your glasses on.
2   TINA: You know perfectly well I can see without them.
3   MAGGIE: Well, I hate to say this in front of Mr. Collier, Tina.
4   TINA: Say what? What are you driving at?
5   MAGGIE: You've just invited the train brakeman home for
6   dinner. *(Blackout)*
7
8
9
10
11
12
13
14
15
16
17
18
19
20
21
22
23
24
25
26
27
28
29
30
31
32
33
34
35

Allowance for Change

Cast of Characters

KAY PATTERSON

Pretty, sensible, conscientious, able to stand on her own feet. Age 32, a social studies teacher in Jefferson City High School.

JEFF BRADLEY

Handsome, muscular, hair starting to grey, wide smile. Age 48, editor of the Jefferson City News. Projects authority and assurance.

VAN DYKE, BENTON and KEEFER

School board members. They all want their own way and by turns, are fussy, eager, interested, kind, old and young.

1   *AT RISE:*   A school board meeting in one of the rooms at Jefferson
2   City High School. A long "board" table and chairs or school
3   desks are scattered about. When the scene opens, KAY
4   PATTERSON is being questioned. The board members, VAN
5   DYKE, BENTON and KEEFER, are dissatisfied. Also present
6   is JEFF BRADLEY, covering the meeting for his paper. JEFF
7   is missing nothing in the interrogation.
8
9   VAN DYKE: Miss Patterson, you understand why you've
10   been called before the school board tonight?
11 BENTON: *(Fussily)* You're a new teacher in Jefferson City,
12   Miss Patterson. Our board has certain policies.
13 KAY: Well, naturally, gentlemen ... and I want to cooperate
14   ... I mean —
15 KEEFER: You teach civics in the tenth grade, Miss Patterson?
16 KAY: Yes, I do, Mr. Keefer.
17 KEEFER: We hired you as an experienced teacher. Shouldn't
18   an experienced teacher know she's better off sticking to
19   the facts in the book? You *have* adequate textbooks?
20 KAY: Oh, yes ... and I use the text all the time.
21 KEEFER: Then why get the children excited about other
22   things? Do you know they're carrying stories home to
23   their parents about what you've said in class?
24 BENTON: One must be guarded in what one says before the
25   young.
26 KAY: But what have I said? I can't think of anything —
27 KEEFER: You mean you aren't aware of what you're teaching?
28 KAY: *(Getting nervous)* No. Yes. Yes, of course I'm aware of
29   what I'm doing.
30 KEEFER: Miss Patterson, just how much do you know about
31   local housing conditions? The so-called slums in
32   Jefferson City you tell your classes about?
33 KAY: *(Flounders. Her hand movements become broader.)* Well — I
34   — ah — I've seen the poorer sections. I mean those houses
35   on Cherry Lane. They're the ones I mentioned.

1　VAN DYKE:　I believe — and correct me if I'm wrong —
2　　　　　you referred to those houses as firetraps.
3　KAY:　Yes, I did, but —
4　KEEFER:　Exactly. By what authority do you make a
5　　　　　statement like that?
6　KAY:　Well, by no authority. Except that I've seen the houses.
7　　　　　I've been through them.
8　BENTON:　And where do firetraps fit into civics?
9　KAY:　We study model housing, Mr. Benton. I pointed out
10　　　　　those houses as an example of what a progressive town
11　　　　　like Jefferson City should get rid of.
12　KEEFER:　Are you aware of what you're doing? Making a
13　　　　　statement like that. Do you realize the — the owner of
14　　　　　those buildings could get very nasty about your accusations?
15　KAY:　I wasn't thinking about the owners. I was thinking of
16　　　　　the tenants.
17　VAN DYKE:　Miss Patterson, we shouldn't like to discharge a
18　　　　　teacher in the middle of the term like this —
19　KAY:　*(Quickly, a little frightened.)* Oh, but that's unfair! I need
20　　　　　this job. I mean —
21　KEEFER:　You're acquainted with the school board's privilege
22　　　　　of blacklisting a teacher in the state?
23　KAY:　*(Near tears)* I — I felt I was doing the right thing.
24　　　　　Something that needed to be done.
25　KEEFER:　You think mud-slinging in the classroom is the
26　　　　　right thing? Is that your conception of a good teacher?
27　KAY:　I wanted to tell the children about better housing.
28　　　　　Certainly you can't fire me for that. You — you wouldn't!
29　VAN DYKE:　No, we shouldn't like to fire you — especially
30　　　　　under these conditions —
31　JEFF:　Look boys, do you mind if I say something right here?
32　KEEFER:　Yes, we would mind, Jeff. You're covering the
33　　　　　meeting for the newspaper. That's all.
34　JEFF:　Now, Sam, not so highhanded.
35　KEEFER:　Editor or no editor, Jeff, this is our business.

1 JEFF: Only Miss Patterson happens to be right. Those
2   properties on Cherry Lane are a disgrace to the
3   community.
4 KEEFER: You and I can talk about that later, Jeff. Right now —
5 JEFF: And if I remember correctly, Sam, you have more than
6   just a — should I say — academic — interest in this.
7 KEEFER: *(Squaring his jaw)* Meaning what?
8 JEFF: Meaning that your brother, Ed, owns that property on
9   Cherry Lane, doesn't he?
10 KEEFER: Let's stick to the facts, Jeff. Leave Ed out of this.
11 JEFF: This wouldn't be a very nice story for the newspaper,
12   gentlemen. School board being used to gag its teachers.
13   Strong-arm technique. That's the way dictators operate,
14   isn't it?
15 VAN DYKE: You wouldn't print a story like that about the
16   school board, Mr. Bradley.
17 JEFF: Well, I wouldn't like to hear of Miss Patterson being
18   fired. Now to me — she seems to be the kind of teacher
19   there ought to be more of around here.
20 VAN DYKE: Sam — ah — maybe we should give the whole
21   matter — ah — further consideration.
22 KEEFER: Jeff, we could have been a little hasty.
23 JEFF: Well, I think I'll chase along now, boys.
24 KEEFER: Now, wait a minute, Jeff. You can't leave yet.
25 JEFF: Why not?
26 KEEFER: Well — we've changed our minds. In regards to
27   Miss Patterson.
28 JEFF: Now, that's what I call progressive thinking, boys.
29   Let's get on with the meeting, shall we? *(Blackout)*
30   *(A corridor in the school building immediately after the meeting.*
31   *A sign, "No Running in Hallways" is prominently displayed.*
32   *JEFF comes on, loosening his tie, and right behind him, KAY*
33   *PATTERSON. We hear the staccato of high heels.)*
34 KAY: Oh, Mr. Bradley. Just a minute, please.
35 JEFF: Congratulations, Miss Patterson.

1	KAY:	Oh, but I don't deserve them. And I want to thank you
2		for what you did tonight. You were splendid.
3	JEFF:	Go ahead. You go on teaching model housing, Miss
4		Patterson. Jefferson City can use it.
5	KAY:	I need this job so badly. You see, I'm helping put my
6		brother through medical school.
7	JEFF:	Glad I was of assistance.
8	KAY:	They were right about that blacklist. They could have
9		done it. That would kill me as a teacher for good.
10	JEFF:	Don't get the board wrong. They're a pretty fair bunch
11		usually. Only you were stepping on somebody's toes, and
12		somebody was putting on the pressure. I just exerted a
13		little counter-pressure, that's all.
14	KAY:	Well, thanks again. I'm really grateful for all you've
15		done. Maybe sometime I'll be able to repay you.
16	JEFF:	Forget it. *(Opens door. Wind and rain pour in. He hastily*
17		*closes door.)* Wow. Look at that rain.
18	KAY:	Good night, Mr. Bradley.
19	JEFF:	Hey, wait a second. I have my car.
20	KAY:	No, no. I can't trouble you any further.
21	JEFF:	Look Miss Patterson, I enjoy a good scrap. And I'll
22		back up what I believe in every time — regardless. That's
23		not trouble. That's the way I work. Now, come along. I'll
24		take you home.
25	KAY:	You know — you know, Mr. Bradley, you're really a
26		very fine person.
27	JEFF:	Thanks. Do we have to be so formal? The name's Jeff.
28	KAY:	I'm Catherine. But I like Kay better.
29	JEFF:	All right, Kay, can I see you home?
30	KAY:	Thank you. I'd — I'd like that, Jeff. *(Blackout)*
31		
32		
33		
34		
35		

Mamma's Boy

Cast of Characters

ALFRED HOGARTH

Age 22, good-looking, muscular (works in a steel mill). Would love to be an adventurer, but has set aside his wishes in deference to his mother's ideas. Genuinely in love with Ruthie.

MRS. HOGARTH

Alfred's mother, about 60. Plain, not interested in clothes or cosmetics, a little dumpy, goodhearted, hospitable, warm and caring. Unconsciously smothering Alfred.

REVEREND THOMAS

Wears a dark suit and a clerical collar. Middle-aged, wants to get along.

RUTH VENIZIO

Age 20, high-spirited, pretty, outgoing. Understands Alfred-and-his-mother situation. Impish. A bit of a tease at times.

1	***AT RISE:*** The living room of ALFRED HOGARTH and his mother
2	is typically middle-class America with a possible exception —
3	MRS. HOGARTH is a compulsive fuss-budget. Little doilies are
4	draped over most of the furniture. Stuffed animals are coyly
5	arranged on the chairs. Artificial flowers decorate the wall
6	pictures. Bad taste is not necessarily MRS. HOGARTH's long
7	suit; coyness is, coupled with artsy-craftsy touches. MRS.
8	HOGARTH is a pleasant woman who feels comfortable and
9	possibly safe wearing an apron. ALFRED, her only child, would
10	love to be adventurous, but Mamma wouldn't dream of letting
11	go. MRS. HOGARTH wants her "baby" at home. She would
12	deny this accusation if faced with it, but unable to help herself,
13	she clings to ALFRED. So far, he's gone along with her, but —
14	when the play opens, ALFRED is putting on his jacket, ready
15	to go to work. It is seven a.m. and a grey, rainy day.
16	
17	**MRS. H.:** *(Coming on carrying ALFRED's rain gear)* **Oh, Alfred,**
18	**there you are.**
19	**ALFRED:** **Just getting ready for work, Mamma.**
20	**MRS. H.:** **Here's your rubbers, dear. And your rain hat and**
21	**your umbrella. I told you at breakfast it was going to —**
22	**ALFRED:** **Oh, Mom! You didn't have to —**
23	**MRS. H.:** **Now we don't want to be up all night again with one**
24	**of our horrid colds, do we? You know how you coughed**
25	**the last time.**
26	**ALFRED:** **Oh. Well, thanks, Mom. Thanks. I have to get moving**
27	**now. I have —**
28	**MRS. H.:** **And, Alfred.**
29	**ALFRED:** **Yes?**
30	**MRS. H.:** **Come right home after work. Remember.**
31	**ALFRED:** **But I —**
32	**MRS. H.:** **Reverend Thomas is coming for dinner, dear. I'll**
33	**need help with the salad. There'll be —**
34	**ALFRED:** **He can't be coming tonight! I have a date tonight.**
35	**Ruthie and I are going to —**

1	MRS. H.: Ruthie. Ruthie. Ruthie. Don't you ever think of
2	anything else but that girl?
3	ALFRED: But I promised her. The club's having a dance.
4	MRS. H.: Some other night, dear.
5	ALFRED: She bought a new dress.
6	MRS. H.: Ruth Venizio will wait. And we're not going to insult
7	Reverend Thomas, are we?
8	ALFRED: No, but —
9	MRS. H.: *(Wounded)* All right. If you feel a dance is more
10	important than having your mother look foolish —
11	ALFRED: *(Agonized)* Oh, Mom, for Pete's sake.
12	MRS. H.: I should imagine you'd want to help your mother all
13	you could.
14	ALFRED: All right. All right. We'll talk about it when I come
15	home after work.
16	MRS. H.: There's nothing to talk about. And don't lose your
17	umbrella, dear. Really, sometimes I think you'd lose your
18	head if it weren't fastened on. *(Blackout)*
19	*(A fragment — an anteroom at the steel factory. Factory whistle,*
20	*crowds moving in the background. A chair, coat rack and desk.*
21	*Both ALFRED and RUTH stand to play this scene. RUTH comes*
22	*running in, ALFRED after her.)*
23	ALFRED: *(Calling)* Ruthie. Ruthie. Ruthie, wait a minute.
24	RUTH: Hi ya, Alfred. What's —
25	ALFRED: You promised you wouldn't call me that.
26	RUTH: Forgot. I'm sorry. Hello, Fred.
27	ALFRED: Ruthie, I have something to tell you.
28	RUTH: I know. We're not going to the dance tonight.
29	ALFRED: Why, how did you —
30	RUTH: I didn't expect to go from the beginning.
31	ALFRED: Mom's having Reverend Thomas over for dinner,
32	and —
33	RUTH: And you have to help make the salad?
34	ALFRED: I couldn't help it, Ruthie. Are you angry?
35	RUTH: After the two-hundreth time? Don't be silly. I'm used to it.

1   ALFRED: I couldn't argue with Mother. I —

2   RUTH: It's all right, Freddie.

3   ALFRED: Not Freddie either.

4   RUTH: Fred.

5   ALFRED: But it isn't all right. We're supposed to be engaged.

6   RUTH: Supposed to be is good.

7   ALFRED: Well, gosh, Ruthie, I tried. But she gets so upset if I—

8   RUTH: I said it was all right, didn't I?

9   ALFRED: But you bought a new dress and all.

10   RUTH: Oh, I'll wear the new dress.

11   ALFRED: But I —

12   RUTH: Oh, Mark Remley asked me to go, too.

13   ALFRED: You can't do that.

14   RUTH: Look Fred, I think you're great. I honestly do. You're
15   kind and considerate. But you're twenty-two. I'm twenty-
16   one. We've been going around together for three years.
17   And we're no closer to being engaged than we ever were.

18   ALFRED: Well, sure we are.

19   RUTH: And if your mother has anything to do with it, we
20   never will be.

21   ALFRED: Then I'll tell her tonight. By gosh, I will tell her.

22   RUTH: No you won't. You've said that before, too.

23   ALFRED: It's just that after Dad died . . . You know, Ruthie,
24   his death was such a lingering one. And Mom got used
25   to taking care of him. It seemed to — fill a space in her
26   life. It was strange. I don't think even she realized it.
27   That it was there — the emptiness. The need. *(Pause)*
28   Then — then afterwards — after the funeral and — it was
29   all over, I guess she couldn't stand it somehow. She'd set
30   a way of life for herself and —

31   RUTH: And she latched on to you.

32   ALFRED: I'm afraid so.

33   RUTH: But Fred, that's the part that's wrong. You know that.
34   I'm not heartless. I can understand her. But you can't let
35   her do that to you just because your dad died. Don't you see?

1 ALFRED: Of course. I've always seen. That's the maddening
2   part.
3 RUTH: And —
4 ALFRED: And I've never known what to do. How to proceed.
5   Without hurting her or anyone else.
6 RUTH: *(Rushes to him, embracing him.)* **Oh, you are a dear.**
7 ALFRED: That's the trouble. But tonight . . . .
8 RUTH: We'll go out another time, Fred. Come on, let's hurry,
9   can we? I'm having my hair done in five minutes. *(She*
10   *starts to rush out, stops.)* **Only — one thing —**
11 ALFRED: Which is?
12 RUTH: Don't give my regards to Reverend Thomas. I'm sure
13   he thinks dancing's sinful. *(Both rush off. Blackout.)*
14   *(We come back to the HOGARTH living room. ALFRED has*
15   *just finished playing a piece on the piano. Something classical*
16   *but not too airy-dairy. REVEREND THOMAS is sitting*
17   *listening. MRS. HOGARTH is beaming as if ALFRED were a*
18   *world-famous concert artist.)*
19 REVEREND: Well. That was splendid, young man. Splendid.
20 MRS. H.:   Alfred, now play the new one for Reverend Thomas.
21   You know the one I like. *(Hums)* **Ti-di-di-di-di.**
22 ALFRED: That's enough for one night, Mom.
23 MRS. H.:   Everyone said Alfred could've had a career in
24   music. He has the touch for it. *(Doorbell rings off.)*
25 ALFRED: That must be Sammy. He said he'd call about
26   leaving for work earlier tomorrow morning. Excuse me,
27   please.
28 REVEREND: Certainly, my boy.
29 MRS. H.:   Of course, dear. *(ALFRED exits.)* **Such a good boy,**
30   Reverend.
31 REVEREND: And such a consolation after — after your poor
32   husband passed on, Mrs. Hogarth.
33 MRS. H.:   He was only twelve when Jim — when Jim was
34   taken. Sometimes I think I may have — well, babied him
35   a bit. But really, Reverend, my only son. He was all I had.

1   My whole life!

2   REVEREND: He never did follow up on that job overseas,
3   Mrs. Hogarth?

4   MRS. H.:   The one in the Middle East? With the Peace Corps?

5   REVEREND: Yes.

6   MRS. H.:   He never heard. Which really suited me if you want
7   the truth, Reverend. That part of the world is so — it's
8   nothing but war and killing there.

9   REVEREND: Still, it's odd. As much as the Peace Corps has
10   tried to recruit workers —

11   MRS. H.:   *(A little too hurriedly)* Oh, you know those
12   government agencies. You could wait years till they
13   answered a letter.

14   REVEREND: *(Laughs)* I expect you're right.

15   MRS. H.:   I was just as glad he put that idea out of his head.
16   Took the job here in the steel mill. Manufacturing steel
17   is a worthwhile vocation.

18   REVEREND: Indeed, Mrs. Hogarth. *(Door opens; ALFRED*
19   *bursts in holding a letter, reading.)*

20   MRS. H.:   Was it Sammy, dear?

21   ALFRED: *(Preoccupied reading)* Not really. It was the special
22   delivery letter man. Would you believe — it's a letter from
23   the Peace Corps.

24   MRS. H.:   *(Amazed)* It can't be!

25   ALFRED: *(Quickly)* Why not? *(MRS. H. doesn't answer. She lifts*
26   *her arms in amazement.)*

27   REVEREND: Good news, Alfred?

28   ALFRED: Well, I'm — I'm not sure yet.

29   MRS. H.:   What — what does it say?

30   ALFRED: *(Throws the letter in the air in jubilation.)* They want
31   me! Me, Mom! Hey!

32   MRS. H.:   What do you mean?

33   REVEREND: Well, congratulations, my boy. That's just fine.
34   Now, I really must be going.

35   MRS. H.:   Reverend, wait. Please.

1   REVEREND: But, I'm — you two will want to talk.

2   MRS. H.:   Alfred —

3   ALFRED: They want me to report immediately, Mom.

4   MRS. H.:   *(She isn't frantic, but she could be.)* **What do you mean,**
5   **immediately? You have a job here. Responsibility. Your**
6   **girl is here, Alfred. Your friends. You'd be willing to throw**
7   **all that over just to —**

8   ALFRED: Hey, Mom. I thought you'd be happy.

9   MRS. H.:   Happy? Well, yes, of course.

10   ALFRED: I'll be doing something to help others. That's what
11   you preach in your overseas missions appeal, isn't it,
12   Reverend?

13   REVEREND: *(Taken aback)* Well, yes, my boy, yes. But the
14   church is — you're an individual. That's entirely
15   different. Your mother might —

16   ALFRED: Oh, Mom only wants what's best for me. Right,
17   Mom?

18   MRS. H.:   *(Smiles pathetically.)* **Alfred.**

19   ALFRED: According to this, my first stop as of next Monday
20   will be an orientation center in Baltimore, Maryland, for
21   six weeks. To learn about the people, the language, the
22   customs in the Middle East. After that — well, I guess it
23   could be anywhere. But the funny part is they wonder
24   why I never responded to their first letter. I don't
25   remember any first letter coming here. Do you, Mom?
26   *(Before MRS. H. can answer, blackout.)*
27   *(The HOGARTH living room again the following Monday.*
28   *ALFRED and RUTH. MRS. H. will enter later.)*

29   ALFRED: Ruthie, listen to me. We've only a minute. A taxi'll
30   be here any second.

31   RUTH: Fred, you're not scared, are you? Don't be.

32   ALFRED: No, no. It's not that. It's you I'm worried about.
33   Ruthie, will you wait for me? Will you be here when I get
34   back? I meant to talk about it so many times. The last
35   few days went by so fast. I —

1   RUTH: You never had time.
2   ALFRED: I had to say goodbye to all of Mom's friends. Every
3   night it was a different one.
4   RUTH: But I —
5   ALFRED: I should have done more for you. You never realize
6   a thing like that until — Ruthie, tell me you'll be here
7   waiting for me. You've always been so sure of yourself.
8   That's what I need.
9   RUTH: Fred, don't you see? It would be all wrong.
10 ALFRED: I don't understand.
11 RUTH: You have your mother to lean upon — to need. You
12   always will. I don't want to be the strong one — no girl
13   does. I want to be loved.
14 MRS. H.:   *(Enters with a bag of goodies she presses on ALFRED. She*
15   *places herself between him and RUTH.)* **Darling, there you**
16   **are. You've had your minute with Ruth. Now, it's mother's**
17   **turn.**
18 ALFRED: *(Taxi horn sounds.)* **Aw — wait a minute, Mom.**
19 MRS. H.:   Alfred, there's your taxi!
20 ALFRED: *(Moves to be near RUTH.)* **Ruthie, you'll write?**
21 RUTH: Of course I will.
22 ALFRED: Ruthie, I —
23 RUTH: Goodbye, Fred. Good luck. *(They embrace. MRS. H. waits*
24   *patiently.)*
25 MRS. H.:   *(Sobs)* **My baby. My little baby. Oh, Alfred.**
26 ALFRED: *(Embracing her)* **Don't cry, Mom. Please don't cry.**
27   *(Taxi horn sounds again.)*
28 MRS. H.:   *(Frantically)* **Remember everything I've told you. I'll**
29   **write you every day. I'll send you boxes. Your favorite**
30   **cookies. Do you have your nose drops? And watch your**
31   **diet, Alfred. No fried things. You know how** — *(Another*
32   *horn blast. ALFRED grabs suitcase and dopp kit.)*
33 ALFRED: Goodbye, Mom. Bye, Ruthie. Bye.
34 RUTH: Goodbye, Fred.
35 MRS. H.:   Goodbye, darling. Remember. Goodbye, Alfred. *(He*

rushes out the door. MRS. H. stands by the open door. She is devastated.) **He's such a baby. He is, Ruth. He's never been away from home in his whole life.** *(Sobs)* **My Alfred. My baby.**

RUTH: *(Meaningfully)* **Yes, I know. Your baby** .... *(Blackout)*

The Circle Closes

Cast of Characters

LOTTIE THOMAS

In her late fifties. A shrewd, greedy woman who feels cheated by life. She is unwell, angry at having to work as a cleaning woman and envious of those with better fortune.

MARGARET POMEROY

The sort of woman children openly make fun of and adults whisper about; in her late sixties; reclusive, suspicious, a hoarder, yet, innately clever too.

1   *AT RISE:*   MRS. MARGARET POMEROY's two-room suite in a
2   small-town hotel that has seen better days. A living room and
3   bedroom, both a complete mess. MRS. POMEROY has saved
4   everything she's gotten her hands on for the last twenty-four
5   years. MRS. POMEROY is a faded old woman of about sixty-
6   eight, cheaply and untidily dressed except for a lovely and
7   expensive shawl. For a second, she nestles her cheek against
8   it, gazes into a mirror.
9
10   *(Knock on door. MRS. POMEROY gives no indication of having*
11   *heard. Another knock on door.)*
12 LOTTIE: *(Off)* **Mrs. Pomeroy. It's Lottie Thomas . . . the maid.**
13   *(MRS. POMEROY completely ignores this.)* **Mrs. Pomeroy, I**
14   **have to get in to clean . . .** *(MRS. POMEROY arranges shawl.*
15   *Sound of key in door. Door is thrown open before MRS.*
16   *POMEROY can protest. LOTTIE enters.)* **Hello, Mrs.**
17   **Pomeroy. Guess you didn't hear me.**
18 MRS. POMEROY: *(Rises from sofa quickly, turns, hides her face.)*
19   **What do you mean breaking in here?**
20 LOTTIE: *(Conciliatory)* **Now, Mrs. Pomeroy. You know today's**
21   **the day we clean. Mr. Niles told you on the phone.**
22 MRS. POMEROY: **I won't have you spying on me like this! I'm**
23   **going to report you.**
24 LOTTIE: **You know I wouldn't spy . . . .**
25 MRS. POMEROY: **Then where'd you get the key?**
.26 LOTTIE: **From Mr. Niles. I explained all that to you last time.**
27   **Remember? I have a key to all the rooms in this section.**
28 MRS. POMEROY: **So you can watch me.**
29 LOTTIE: **No, so I can watch out for you. Now, you want me to**
30   **clean up, don't you?**
31 MRS. POMEROY: **You're paid to clean. It's your job.**
32 LOTTIE: **That's right. I'll start in the bedroom, and you can**
33   **sit in here. All right?**
34 MRS. POMEROY: **What are you going to do in there?**
35 LOTTIE: **Clean. I just told you . . . .**

1   MRS. POMEROY: How?

2   LOTTIE: What do you mean, how?

3   MRS. POMEROY: Don't pretend you don't know.

4   LOTTIE: Oh, well, run the sweeper. Dust. Change the bed.

5   MRS. POMEROY: You'll touch things.

6   LOTTIE: No, I promise. *(An idea)* **That is, unless you tell me**

7   **what things you don't want touched.**

8   MRS. POMEROY: That's none of your business.

9   LOTTIE: But if you told me, then —

10 MRS. POMEROY: You get out of here. I don't like you.

11 LOTTIE: Now, Mrs. Pomeroy, don't get upset. You sit here

12   and I'll start.

13 MRS. POMEROY: How long have you been working for me?

14 LOTTIE: Three, four years now . . . .

15 MRS. POMEROY: No, you haven't.

16 LOTTIE: Don't you remember? Mamie had you first. Mamie

17   Stettler. She quit when her legs got bad. Then I started.

18 MRS. POMEROY: You shouldn't lie. *(LOTTIE disappears into*

19   *bedroom.)*

20 LOTTIE: *(Wearily)* **All right. I won't anymore.**

21 MRS. POMEROY: *(Talking after her)* **Because you have to**

22   **work, you want people to feel sorry for you. Oh, yes,**

23   **sympathy's what you're after, but you're not getting it.**

24   **Mamma always said not to sympathize too much with**

25   **people — and I always listened to Mamma.** *(Sounds of*

26   *cleaning in bedroom.)* **You're better than the rest, she said.**

27   **Don't ever forget that.** *(LOTTIE suddenly appears at door in*

28   *act of cleaning.)* **Stop your peeping at me! I won't stand for**

29   **it! I know your tricks.** *(LOTTIE grits her teeth, goes back into*

30   *bedroom, spotlight stays with LOTTIE as MRS. POMEROY*

31   *talks.)* **And see that you don't touch anything in there. I**

32   **don't like my things moved.** *(Pause)* **Do you hear me?**

33   *(LOTTIE doesn't answer. She is frantically searching room.)*

34   **Answer me!**

35 LOTTIE: Yes. Yes.

1　MRS. POMEROY:　The help just don't know their place
2　　　　anymore. They did when I was a girl. Mamma took me
3　　　　downtown and our Clara walked two steps behind us . . . I
4　　　　was such a good girl for Mamma. *(Suddenly high)* I did
5　　　　everything Mamma told me! Everything!
6　　　　*(LOTTIE picks up book, tries to close it when money falls out.*
7　　　　*She is wordless, stoops over to pick it up, realizes how much is*
8　　　　*there — hundreds — just tucked in a book. She goes to bookshelf,*
9　　　　*picks another book at random. There's money in it too.*
10　　　　*Meanwhile, MRS. POMEROY has reached a high note in her*
11　　　　*speech. LOTTIE's eyes shift outside, her hand goes lovingly over*
12　　　　*the money. Temptation is too much. She stuffs a handful of the*
13　　　　*money in her pocket with a sudden gesture. MRS. POMEROY*
14　　　　*appears at doorway and screams.)*
15　MRS. POMEROY:　*(Cont.)* **Put that back, or I'll kill you!** *(LOTTIE*
16　　　　*stands frozen. MRS. POMEROY rushes to table, opens drawer,*
17　　　　*pulls out gun.)*
18　LOTTIE:　*(Screams)* **Oh!**
19　MRS. POMEROY:　Put it back, you thief!
20　LOTTIE:　*(Struggling to get money back)* **No, no! I wasn't going to**
21　　　　take it . . . .
22　MRS. POMEROY:　You were trying to rob me . . . *(Screams)*
23　　　　Help! Help!
24　LOTTIE:　Don't scream. Please! I was just cleaning. I swear!
25　　　　I lifted the book to dust and —
26　MRS. POMEROY:　And you took other things. I saw you.
27　LOTTIE:　No, I didn't. Listen, Mrs. Pomeroy —
28　MRS. POMEROY:　You can give your explanations to the
29　　　　police.
30　LOTTIE:　Please! See, I put the money back. I only picked it
31　　　　up for a second to clean. You know you can trust me. Please.
32　MRS. POMEROY:　*(Considers)* **Well** . . . *(Drops gun by her side.)*
33　　　　Why not? It's only wood. A toy. I don't have a real gun.
34　　　　Fooled you, didn't I? *(She goes into gales of laughter.)*
35　LOTTIE:　A fake gun . . . .

1   **MRS. POMEROY:**   **Guess you won't steal things so fast from**
2   **people now . . .** *(Then, venomously)* **But I don't want you**
3   **cleaning for me anymore.**
4   **LOTTIE:**   *(Suddenly calm. Her plans are beginning to take shape.)*
5   **It's all right, Mrs. Pomeroy. No one can take anything**
6   **while you're here, can they?**
7   **MRS. POMEROY:**   **You tried to . . . .**
8   **LOTTIE:**   **I didn't. Honest! But isn't it dangerous to leave**
9   **money lying around the room like that?**
10   **MRS. POMEROY:**   **I haven't any money here. It's all in the bank.**
11   **LOTTIE:**   **Now, Mrs. Pomeroy. You can trust me.**
12   **MRS. POMEROY:**   **I can't trust anyone!** *(Grows more excited.)*
13   **Not even that man in the kitchen downstairs. He sent up**
14   **poisoned food last night, but I wouldn't eat it. I just kept**
15   **the sugar.** *(Then very mysteriously — pause)* **If you won't say**
16   **anything, I'll show you something wonderful . . .** *(Hope*
17   *lights LOTTIE's face. MRS. POMEROY goes to chest of drawers*
18   *in living room, opens drawer. There are hundreds of sugars in*
19   *wrappers. LOTTIE follows her.)*
20   **LOTTIE:**   **Sugar! Packets of sugar!**
21   **MRS. POMEROY:**   *(Cautions her.)* **Not so loud. They'll hear you.**
22   **They listen.** *(Nods her head yes.)* **Oh, yes. See! And I keep**
23   **all my grocery bags in this other drawer.** *(Pulls out another*
24   *drawer — more money is revealed. She hastily shuts that.)*
25   **LOTTIE:**   *(Her face lights up.)* **Hey, they're not grocery bags.**
26   **MRS. POMEROY:**   **No, the next one.** *(She pulls out another*
27   *drawer, but LOTTIE has lost interest. She looks at MRS.*
28   *POMEROY speculatively, then around room.)* **I keep**
29   **everything neat. That's where my sister Esther and I were**
30   **different.** *(Telephone rings. MRS. POMEROY looks at*
31   *LOTTIE. Telephone rings again.)*
32   **LOTTIE:**   **The telephone's ringing, Mrs. Pomeroy.**
33   **MRS. POMEROY:**   *(Makes no move.)* **I hear it.** *(Telephone rings*
34   *again.)*
35   **LOTTIE:**   **Hadn't you better . . .?**

1   MRS. POMEROY: No one ever phones except my lawyer —
2   and he can wait.
3   LOTTIE: Want me to answer it?
4   MRS. POMEROY: It's my phone. You get out.
5   LOTTIE: All right. I'll be back later.
6   MRS. POMEROY: I don't want you back.
7   LOTTIE: I have to come back . . . for the dirty linen.
8   MRS. POMEROY: I said I don't want you. *(Slams door in her*
9   *face. Telephone rings again. MRS. POMEROY picks it up, looks*
10   *at it, replaces phone. She locks the door and leans against it.*
11   *She's safe! She thinks! Blackout.)*
12
13
14
15
16
17
18
19
20
21
22
23
24
25
26
27
28
29
30
31
32
33
34
35

A Sense of Honor

Cast of Characters

PEG MICHAELS

A beautiful girl of 24 who has used her beauty to take what she wants from life. Unfortunately, she doesn't know what this is, only that she is driven, restless, and willing to do what she needs to satisfy her desires.

FRANK MICHAELS

Peg's husband, nice-looking, 26. Generous and hard working, the type of man who sees only the best in everyone and who would go to any length to protect his home and his wife.

1　***AT RISE:***　The kitchen of the Michaels' house in a small coal mining
2　　　　　　town in Pennsylvania. A large room, it serves almost as a living
3　　　　　　room. A studio couch and a rocker along with a table and chairs
4　　　　　　and other kitchen equipment. It is nicely kept. The door opens
5　　　　　　and FRANK MICHAELS enters. Outside the weather is
6　　　　　　nasty — rain, wind blowing. FRANK picks up the evening
7　　　　　　newspaper, then wipes his feet on the mat outside before
8　　　　　　entering. He is wearing a raincoat, turned up at the collar, and
9　　　　　　is carrying a small package. As he enters, he calls.
10
11　**FRANK:**　**Peg?** *(No answer. He turns on the light and calls again.)*
12　　　　　**Honey, you home?** *(Still no answer. He lays his package and*
13　　　　　*newspaper on table, then takes off raincoat, throws it over a*
14　　　　　*kitchen chair.)* **Hey, honey!** *(There is still no answer. He walks*
15　　　　　*to the door leading to the rest of the house, opens it, flicks on*
16　　　　　*another light.)* **Peg. You sleeping?**
17　　　　　*(He walks off set. He is only gone a second, comes back into*
18　　　　　*kitchen and goes to table, opening his newspaper. He stands*
19　　　　　*there, newspaper on table, reading it, abstractedly pulling his*
20　　　　　*tie down and loosening his shirt collar. Then he picks up*
21　　　　　*newspaper, continues to read as he takes off suit coat which he*
22　　　　　*throws on studio couch. He continues reading when suddenly he*
23　　　　　*looks out window. Rain pouring against the pane. He goes to*
24　　　　　*stove and shakes coffeepot. There is coffee in it, but to make sure,*
25　　　　　*he opens lid and looks. Satisfied, he turns on stove to heat coffee,*
26　　　　　*finally puts paper down to go to cupboard for a cup and saucer.*
27　　　　　*He is getting a cup when the door opens and PEG enters quickly,*
28　　　　　*closing the door behind her. She leans against it, glances down*
29　　　　　*at the floor and takes a deep breath. FRANK whirls.)*
30　**FRANK:**　*(Cont.)* **Hi, honey.** *(She doesn't answer, and he stares at*
31　　　　　*her.)* **Peg, what's wrong?** *(PEG still doesn't answer. She is*
32　　　　　*quick and sudden in her movements. There is a lushness about*
33　　　　　*her beauty. She is breathing hard, obviously working furiously*
34　　　　　*to control herself. Suddenly, she looks up and smiles.)*
35　**PEG:**　**Nothing. You just get home, Frank?**

1 FRANK: Few minutes ago. Where were you? Shopping? *(PEG*
2   *comes into room, taking off her coat which she takes out into*
3   *other room, talking as she goes.)*
4 PEG: No. Blanche called . . . she wanted to see the movie at
5   the Grand.
6 FRANK: In this weather?
7 PEG: Sure. Why not?
8 FRANK: What'd you do? Take the car?
9 PEG: *(Suddenly high)* What difference does it make? Why
10   shouldn't I take it?
11 FRANK: No reason, honey. *(Pause)* What's the matter?
12   Anything wrong?
13 PEG: I'm just sick of being cross-examined every day, about
14   every last detail. Where'd you go? What'd you do? You'd
15   think I was a kid . . . .
16 FRANK: Something happen to the car, Peg?
17 PEG: *(Turns to him suddenly)* All right. Something did happen.
18 FRANK: You smash it?
19 PEG: No . . . *(FRANK waits.)* Frank, you know I need three
20   spaces at the curb to park. Market Street was jammed,
21   so I circled around the block. When I got to Fourth and
22   Arch, I didn't see the red light. Blanche yelled, and I
23   jammed on the brakes, but —
24 FRANK: Go into a spin?
25 PEG: *(She is getting panicky.)* I don't know . . . it . . . it
26   happened so fast, and Blanche was screaming — I could
27   hardly see, it was raining so . . . .
28 FRANK: But what happened?
29 PEG: *(Desperate, near tears)* Frank, I'm trying to tell you! I . . . I
30   hit someone. I hit a man! *(She gasps, suddenly breaks down,*
31   *then runs to him and buries her head against him. He allows*
32   *her to rest there a second.)*
33 FRANK: *(Gently)* Honey, sit down. *(He leads her to sofa. She sits. He*
34   *goes to stove, turns off heat on coffee.)* Here, the coffee's hot now.
35 PEG: No . . I can't . . . It . . . it was horrible . . . *(She puts her*

1 *hands over her mouth a second.)* **I caught him with the**
2 **bumper.**
3 FRANK: **Who was he?**
4 PEG: **I ... I don't know ....**
5 FRANK: **You don't know? But you must!**
6 PEG: *(After a pause)* **I didn't stop.**
7 FRANK: *(Aghast)* **You what!?**
8 PEG: *(Jumps up.)* **Now don't start yelling at me. I ... I was**
9 **afraid. I thought maybe he was dead. So I — backed up**
10 **and drove away.**
11 FRANK: **And left him lying there?**
12 PEG: **I tell you I was afraid! Blanche said it was all right.**
13 **Nobody saw us.**
14 FRANK: **What does that matter?**
15 PEG: **Frank, can't you understand ...?** *(He turns away, comes*
16 *to a decision.)*
17 FRANK: **All right. I can understand ... I guess.** *(He turns back*
18 *to her.)* **When did it happen?**
19 PEG: **How can I ....**
20 FRANK: *(Sharply)* **Peg! Answer me!**
21 PEG: **About ... twenty minutes ago. It was around ten after**
22 **five. I looked at my watch.**
23 FRANK: **You're sure?**
24 PEG: **We got out of the movie at five ... Frank! Why do you**
25 **want to know? You ... you won't go to the police? They'll**
26 **put me in jail.**
27 FRANK: *(Starts for his coat.)* **I'm only trying to help.**
28 PEG: *(Frantic)* **I couldn't see! That intersection is built up on**
29 **all sides.**
30 FRANK: **The one at Fourth and Arch? Right?** *(FRANK pulls*
31 *up tie, grabs suit coat, puts it on.)*
32 PEG: **What are you going to do? Frank, where are you going?**
33 *(FRANK doesn't answer. Gets raincoat and puts it on.)*
34 **No ... You can't go out now! I won't stay alone.**
35 FRANK: **Honey, I've got to go back and see what happened to**

1   **that man.**

2 **PEG:** *(Screams)* **Frank!**

3 **FRANK:** *(Gently)* **Honey, don't. It'll be all right. I promise**

4   **you. It'll be all right.** *(He leaves. Her sobbing increases. Fade*

5   *out.)*

6

7

8

9

10

11

12

13

14

15

16

17

18

19

20

21

22

23

24

25

26

27

28

29

30

31

32

33

34

35

Edge of Danger

Cast of Characters

MARY PALSANO

A woman in love with the wrong man. She is 35, driven, plain, so eager to please. She is growing desperate.

CHARLES BRENNER

About 25, very good-looking and very macho (he thinks); an opportunist willing to let others do the work and he'll pick up the benefits. He is wearing only trousers, no clothes above the waist, bare feet.

1	*AT RISE:* Living room of MARY's home. The furniture is clumsy
2	and worn. CHARLES BRENNER is lying on sofa, drinking beer
3	and watching television. The door opens and CHARLES quickly
4	springs to his feet. When he sees who it is, he relaxes. MARY
5	is carrying a huge load of groceries. He makes no move to help
6	her. She puts grocery bag on table.
7	
8	CHARLES: Oh, it's you.
9	MARY: *(Genuinely in love)* Hi, darling.
10	CHARLES: Need help?
11	MARY: *(Fussing with groceries)* It's OK. I can manage.
12	CHARLES: You didn't forget I need cigarettes and a six-pack?
13	MARY: *(Smiling)* Think I want to lose my happy home?
14	*(Hands him carton. He takes it without comment.)* Well,
15	don't I rate a kiss? *(They embrace, then he goes back to*
16	*sofa.)*
17	CHARLES: I thought maybe it was that cleaning woman
18	coming back.
19	MARY: Ethel? She finished at four, didn't she?
20	CHARLES: Yeah, I guess.
21	MARY: You paid her, didn't you, Charlie? I left the money in
22	the cupboard.
23	CHARLES: I got it.
24	MARY: *(Pause, hesitantly)* But — did you, Charlie?
25	CHARLES: Did I what? *(She looks at him.)* I — needed some
26	things. You're not going to nag me over a couple of bucks.
27	MARY: But, you promised —
28	CHARLES: All right. I spent it. You try laying around this
29	dump all day . . . .
30	MARY: You — you didn't see about that job at Thornton
31	Products?
32	CHARLES: I called. *(MARY waits.)* They're not hiring.
33	MARY: The newspaper ad said —
34	CHARLES: Can't you get it through your head? I don't want
35	factory work. You're talking to Charlie Brenner now.

1   *(MARY waits.)* **Besides, you might as well know.**

2 **MARY:**   **Honey, what's wrong?**

3 **CHARLES:**   **What's the use? I won't be around that long.**

4 **MARY:** *(Suddenly panicky)* **Charlie, don't kid like that.**

5 **CHARLES:**   **Who's kidding? I'm wasting my time around here.**

6   **Yesterday, I heard about a deal I'd like to latch onto in**

7   **Atlantic City.**

8 **MARY:**   **Atlantic City . . .?**

9 **CHARLES:**   **That's right.**

10 **MARY:**   **But, Charlie . . . you can't go. I . . . I won't let you.**

11 **CHARLES:**   **You won't let me? Look. Back off. I'm not your**

12   **husband, Mary. I'm just the roomer. In the bedroom at**

13   **the end of the hall. Second door to the right.**

14 **MARY:** *(Anguished)* **Charlie. Please —**

15 **CHARLES:**   **I'll be pretty sorry to leave you — you know that**

16   **but, honey, I can't scratch along on free room and board**

17   **and a measly twenty or thirty bucks a week —**

18 **MARY:** *(Tense)* **Charlie, sit down — please —**

19 **CHARLES:** *(After a momentary pause, he does.)* **Well?**

20 **MARY:**   **I've got to talk to you — I want you to understand,**

21   **Charlie. I never had anything before you came along.**

22   **When I was a kid — for six years — Poppa was sick. After**

23   **that, living alone here with Momma — you don't know**

24   **what it was like. She nagged night and day. I never went**

25   **anywhere or saw anyone. Even after she died — but then**

26   **you moved in — and for the first time in my life, I had**

27   **something that was mine. No, I'm not going to lose it,**

28   **Charlie. I won't lose it, no matter what I have to do!**

29 **CHARLES:**   **I don't see how you can help yourself, honey —**

30 **MARY:** *(This is hard to say.)* **It's . . . money you want . . . isn't it?**

31 **CHARLES:**   **Well, a guy's got to live . . .**

32 **MARY:** *(Almost a whisper)* **All right. You'll have money . . . I'll**

33   **give it to you . . . .**

34 **CHARLES:**   **Look, I told you. A few bucks a week won't . . . .**

35 **MARY:**   **It'll be more than that. It'll be . . . a great deal more . . . .**

1   CHARLES: Yeah?

2   MARY: Maybe ... a couple of hundred dollars. Every week ....

3   CHARLES: Where could you get that kind of dough?

4   MARY: *(Bitterly)* **Does it matter as long as I get it?**

5   CHARLES: **What are you going to do? Murder somebody?**

6   MARY: *(She rises, goes to table where she left her purse, opens it*

7   *and   pulls   out   bills.)*   **I've   already   got — the   first**

8   **installment ...**   *(CHARLES watches her goggle-eyed. She*

9   *counts out the bills on the table. Blackout.)*

10

11

12

13

14

15

16

17

18

19

20

21

22

23

24

25

26

27

28

29

30

31

32

33

34

35

What's in a Name?

Cast of Characters

NANCY MARSHALL

About 24, pretty, serious, restrained; doesn't want to hurt anyone's feelings. Thoroughly likeable; the town's librarian.

BOB CRAWFORD

Twenty-eight, handsome, sure of himself (but not cocky); a successful businessman, knows what he wants; book publisher.

DEAN MARSHALL

Nancy's father, 55, but grumps around as if he were 75; fussy, abstracted.

REX FARRADAY

About 35, good-looking, slick, extra neat dresser; turns on the charm when needed.

MARTHA DEANS

Single, 45, but thinks of herself as 22; fluttery, easily flattered, likes the men.

1	***AT RISE:*** Two offices, side by side, with a connecting door between
2	them. One office, the Crawford Publishing Company in New
3	York, features smart, up-to-date office furniture, and to provide
4	a sense of locale, posters advertising New York plays and a new
5	book coming out. The second office has a run-down academic
6	air. An old desk piled with papers, telephone, file cabinet, book
7	cases, and on the walls, collegiate pennants and framed
8	diplomas. The actress playing NANCY MARSHALL will move
9	between the two adjoining rooms through the connecting door.
10	
11	**BOB:** *(At desk of New York office, rises as NANCY enters from*
12	*outside door.)* **Well, Nancy Marshall — my favorite writer**
13	**and my favorite blonde. Come in.**
14	**NANCY:** **Hello, Bob. How are you?**
15	**BOB:** *(Walks toward her, takes her coat, puts it on a chair, then*
16	*takes both her hands.)* **Well, speaking as your publisher, I've**
17	**been getting darned impatient for the last three chapters**
18	**of "The Lincoln City Story." As a fellow who hasn't seen**
19	**his girl in a long time, I think I'd enjoy a welcome kiss.**
20	**NANCY:** *(A little shocked.)* **Oh, Bob, don't say things like that.**
21	**BOB:** *(Moving a step closer to her)* **Why do you always get so**
22	**shocked every time I suggest kissing you? I'm single,**
23	**presentable, and twenty-eight.**
24	**NANCY:** *(Taking one step backwards)* **But you make me blush.**
25	**Lincoln City isn't like New York.**
26	**BOB:** *(Edging closer)* **Well, one kiss isn't going to turn you into**
27	**a bad little girl. I promise.**
28	**NANCY:** **I think we'd better talk about the book, hadn't we?**
29	**BOB:** **I think we could combine business and pleasure. Like**
30	**this.** *(He kisses her.)*
31	**NANCY:** *(She enjoys it but thinks she shouldn't. Pause; gasps.)* **Bob!**
32	**BOB:** **I'll have you know I don't make love to every writer who**
33	**comes in here.**
34	**NANCY:** **I don't know half the time whether you're serious**
35	**or not.**

1　BOB:　Well, I could be serious about you. But maybe we'd
2　　　　better get to work. Where are those last three chapters?
3　NANCY:　That's just it, Bob. They're not finished.
4　BOB:　Why, what's the matter? You'd planned those chapters
5　　　　on — now, let's see — one was going to be about a college
6　　　　dean — that'd be your father. Right?
7　NANCY:　Yes.
8　BOB:　And then two other people in Lincoln City.
9　NANCY:　Rex Farraday — he's a real estate agent and too darn
10　　　　slick to suit me — and Martha Deans — she's kind of a
11　　　　flutter-budget.
12　BOB:　OK, we've got that much settled. Now, what's the next
13　　　　problem?
14　NANCY:　I don't know how to begin. I mean —
15　BOB:　*(Ushers her to an easy chair.)* **Look, why can't we be**
16　　　　**comfortable while we're discussing this?** *(NANCY sits.)*
17　　　　**I'll get us some coffee.** *(He exits through outside door, speaking*
18　　　　*as he goes. Offstage:)* **You drink it black, don't you?** *(Returns*
19　　　　*with two cups of coffee, gives NANCY one.)*
20　NANCY:　That'll be fine.
21　BOB:　*(Sits behind his desk.)* **Now, we can lean back and**
22　　　　**really let go.**
23　NANCY:　All right. I'll tell you what the people are like — then
24　　　　maybe you can suggest what I can do with them. *(Sighs)*
25　　　　Oh, dear, being a librarian is so much easier on the nerves
26　　　　than writing a book. Particularly under the pen name of
27　　　　C. C. Carlyle. Honestly.
28　BOB:　All right. Where shall we start?
29　NANCY:　Well, you do know that Dad's on the university
30　　　　faculty —
31　BOB:　You told me that.
32　NANCY:　Well, he's sort of an old — well, old and grumpy I
33　　　　guess you'd say. Anyway, that's what the students call
34　　　　him behind his back — God love him. I mean, this is the
35　　　　kind of things he does. The other day, I went down to his

1	office, and he was looking all over the place for some
2	papers. *(As NANCY talks, lights fade on New York office and*
3	*come up on the university office.)*
4	*(DEAN MARSHALL is discovered looking all over the place for*
5	*his papers. NANCY enters through connecting door, speaking*
6	*as she walks.)*
7	NANCY: *(Cont.)* **Hi ya, Pops. What are you doing? Tearing**
8	**your office apart?**
9	DEAN: *(Fussily)* **Oh, hello, dear. It's that incompetent Miss**
10	**Sylvester again. She always hides things so I can't find**
11	**them. She must think I have all day to play hide-and-seek.**
12	NANCY: **What'd you lose?**
13	DEAN: **My Latin examination papers. And I just had them.**
14	NANCY: **Did you look in your files?**
15	DEAN: **Certainly I looked in my files. Where do you think I'd**
16	**look?**
17	NANCY: *(Thumbs through file cabinet.)* **Let *me* see. Why, here**
18	**they are. Under the "L's".**
19	DEAN: **Now, isn't that just like her. Filing Latin papers**
20	**under "L".**
21	NANCY: **Well, where would you put them?**
22	DEAN: **Under "P". For papers. Anyone would know that. It**
23	**seems to me that if that girl —** *(Telephone rings; continuing*
24	*anyway)* **— would put things where I could find them, I**
25	**could cut the time in half that I spend in this office. I**
26	**mean exactly that. In half.** *(Telephone again; oblivious.)* **I**
27	**never got mixed up before Miss Sylvester came.**
28	NANCY: **Dean, your telephone's ringing.**
29	DEAN: **Oh! Oh, so it is.** *(Lifts receiver.)* **Hello . . . Oh, hello, Coach**
30	**Parkansky . . . Yes, I've corrected Biff Stewart's Latin**
31	**paper . . . Well, to be frank with you, Coach, that young**
32	**man may be a good athlete, but you know what he made**
33	**in Latin? . . . He made seventeen. I gave him that since**
34	**he had his own name and the name of the course spelled**
35	**right. Outside of that . . . well, now, Coach, you can't expect**

1	me to pass the man merely to let him play football, can
2	you? ... Oh, you can ... Well, no, I don't see how he can
3	have a re-examination ... Very well, we'll discuss it
4	later ... Yes, goodbye. *(Replaces receiver.)* **Can you imagine**
5	**that, Nancy? Wanting me to give Biff Stewart a re-**
6	**examination so he can play on the football team. Football,**
7	**indeed.**
8	NANCY: **But Dad, Biff's the best player they have. Couldn't**
9	**you give him a little leeway?**
10	DEAN: **Leeway? Do you know what he's done so far in my**
11	**classes? Sleep or rattle newspapers. The comic sections.**
12	**It's high time this nonsense about pampering athletes**
13	**stops.**
14	NANCY: **But after all, it gives the university a reputation**
15	**and —**
16	DEAN: **And if I get the presidency of the university, as I hope**
17	**to, I will stop it. You can count on that.**
18	NANCY: **Oh, Dad, don't be so — so fussy about it. I mean —**
19	DEAN: **Fussy, my hat. Now, run along, Nancy. I have work to**
20	**do. I have to look over my ancient Greek papers — if I**
21	**can ever find them.**
22	NANCY: **Well, look in the right place for a change, Dad.**
23	DEAN: **I certainly will. I'm going to look under the "A's" —**
24	**for ancient.**
25	*(Lights dim and go up on New York office as the DEAN speaks.*
26	*NANCY exits into New York office. BOB is laughing.)*
27	NANCY: **You see, Bob, that's the sort of thing I mean.**
28	BOB: *(Still laughing)* **Write it just as you've told it to me, Nancy.**
29	**It'll be perfect.**
30	NANCY: **Of course, the other two aren't that easy.**
31	BOB: **That's right. Now, who are they?**
32	NANCY: **Well, Rex Farraday — the real estate agent, and**
33	**Miss Deans.** *(Imitating her)* **Dear Martha.** *(Normal)* **She's in**
34	**a constant dither.**
35	BOB: **What are they like?**

1   **NANCY:** *(As she speaks, lights go down again on New York office*
2   *and come up on university office.)* **Well, I'll just tell you.**
3   **They're both on the library board. And we were meeting**
4   **in Dad's office the other night about buying some books.**
5   *(REX and MARTHA are discovered. NANCY enters through*
6   *connecting door.)*
7   **REX:** *(Slick and pompous. Holds out books for NANCY's inspection*
8   *as she enters room.)* **Now, here's my selection, Miss Nancy.**
9   **All fine titles. And all books to build citizenship for the**
10   **youth of Lincoln City.**
11   **NANCY:** But Mr. Farraday —
12   **MARTHA:** Oh, Rex is right, Nancy. We must build — build —
13   build the minds of the young. That's what I tell my camp
14   fire girls.
15   **NANCY:** I was only going to say, Miss Deans, we seem to have
16   so many of these books already. And none of the children
17   are very interested in them.
18   **REX:** You must make them aware of their duty as little citizens,
19   Miss Nancy.
20   **MARTHA:** Oh, you must, Nancy. In times like these, it's very
21   important to be — ah — ah — patriotic. Yes. Very
22   important.
23   **NANCY:** Well, all right, if that's what you want.
24   **REX:** You see, Miss Nancy, being in the real estate business
25   like I am, I come into contact with all types. I realize the
26   value of early training.
27   **MARTHA:** Which reminds me, Rex. Mrs. Potter wants to meet
28   you. I was telling her about that perfectly wonderful
29   property you're selling — you know, those silver mine
30   things out west, and I believe she wants to invest too.
31   **REX:** Well, now, Martha, that was generous of you. *(Licking his*
32   *chops.)* Mrs. Potter, eh. Quite a wealthy woman, isn't she?
33   **MARTHA:** And a widow, too, Rex. Now, don't you get any
34   romantic ideas about her.
35   **REX:** Well, I'm sure she won't have your charm, my dear. In

| 1 | the year I've been in Lincoln City, I have yet to meet a |
| 2 | woman quite like you. |

1   the year I've been in Lincoln City, I have yet to meet a
2   woman quite like you.
3 MARTHA: Oh, I've just loved every minute of introducing
4   you around.
5 NANCY: Incidentally, Mr. Farraday, didn't you sell my dad
6   some of that western real estate — the silver mining
7   business Miss Deans mentioned?
8 REX: Yes, indeed, your father put a thousnd dollars in that
9   land. A very shrewd investment too. Those lots have been
10   going like hot cakes all over Lincoln City.
11 NANCY: And has anyone found silver on the land yet?
12 REX: Not yet, but those things take time, Miss Marshall. New
13   development, you know. Always a slow process. But we'd
14   better get back to the business at hand, hadn't we?
15 MARTHA: Oh, dear, yes. I have two more meetings
16   scheduled for tonight — those European relief societies.
17   Very worthwhile.
18 REX: Now, here's a fine title — "More and More Geography
19   for Children."
20 NANCY: We have six copies of that already.
21 REX: Order six more. Can't have too many of that book.
22 MARTHA: You know, I was just thinking. At my Chinese relief
23   meeting tonight, I'm going to suggest buying pins for the
24   members. White and gold enamel with dragons on them.
25   Doesn't that sound exciting?
26 REX: Martha, you're doing a fine job with your socieites.
27   Very public spirited.
28 MARTHA: Oh, Rex, how kind of you. It's only my duty. We
29   must build for the future, you know.
30   *(Lights are going down on university office and coming up on*
31   *New York office as the talk goes on.)*
32 NANCY: *(Patiently)* Shall we get on with the book ordering?
33   *(Enters New York office through connecting door.)* You see,
34   Bob, they're both such phonies.
35 BOB: Seems to me as if you could do a pretty good job on

1   those two, Nancy.
2   NANCY: In the book, I'm going to call Rex Old King Gold.
3   You can't tell me that silver mining property is on the
4   up and up.
5   BOB: What makes you so sure?
6   NANCY: Well, Rex's approach, for one thing. He's too slick to
7   suit me. And nobody's seen a cent of profit on their
8   investments. He's obviously using Miss Deans for his own
9   purposes — and she just never catches on.
10   BOB: By the way, I have a name for her — Miss Featherstone.
11   NANCY: Wonderful. It just suits.
12   BOB: Well, think you're all straightened out now, Nancy?
13   NANCY: You know, I believe I am. Just talking it out with you
14   helps so much.
15   BOB: It's going to be a good book, Nancy, and I'd like to see
16   you get credit for it. Why don't you reconsider and
17   publish it under your own name?
18   NANCY: But I wouldn't dare. Not that I'd be afraid to stand
19   behind what I've written — but you know Dad's being
20   considered for the university presidency. The board of
21   trustees would have a fit if they knew I'd written a book
22   like "The Lincoln City Story."
23   BOB: I doubt it.
24   NANCY: Well, Bob, they would. I've even poked fun at my
25   own father in it.
26   BOB: But if the book's the success I know it's going to be, you
27   can quit your librarian's job anyway. You'll want to spend
28   all your time writing, or maybe —
29   NANCY: Bob, let's not argue about it again. That book is being
30   written by C. C. Carlyle. You agreed to it in my contract.
31   BOB: Oh, Nancy, can't you see I'm trying to pull you out of
32   that little shell you seem to crawl into. You're so afraid
33   of what will hurt your dad — or what is and what isn't
34   proper according to Lincoln City — Nancy, stand on your
35   own two feet. Grow up.

1	NANCY: *(Miffed)* I rather thought I was grown up. Some
2	people think I am.
3	BOB: Well, I'm not one of them.
4	NANCY: I don't see where it makes so much difference to you.
5	You're my publisher — not my —
6	BOB: Not your boyfriend?
7	NANCY: I didn't say that.
8	BOB: No, but you meant it.
9	NANCY: Of all the outrageous conceit!
10	BOB: It isn't conceit. It's the truth. And I'll tell you something
11	else, Miss Nancy Marshall of Lincoln City — I could be
12	in love with you —
13	NANCY: *(Gasps)* Bob!
14	BOB: Does that surprise you? Well, it's the truth. But when I
15	fall in love, it's going to be with a girl who isn't afraid — a
16	girl that I can stand back and admire.
17	NANCY: Well, thanks. Are you finished now, Bob Crawford?
18	BOB: Not quite.
19	NANCY: Oh, yes, you are. I'm going back to Lincoln City
20	tonight. You can let me know when the book comes out.
21	Goodbye, Mr. Crawford.
22	BOB: *(Tries to restrain her.)* Nancy, wait.
23	NANCY: Bob, let go of me.
24	BOB: All right, if that's the way you feel. Give my love to the
25	volumes back in your library, Nancy. Particularly to the
26	collection of "More and More Geography for Children."
27	NANCY: *(She starts out.)* I certainly will. Goodbye. *(She exits*
28	*through outer door. BOB stands there a second, throws his pencil*
29	*on his desk in disgust, slumps in his chair. Blackout.)*
30	
31	
32	
33	
34	
35	

The Brass Ring

Cast of Characters

MARGO RICHARDS
*Twenty-five, striking, thin; a little "actressy,"
different, nice, warm, generous-hearted.*

CLIPPER MADISON
*Twenty-three, "farm boy in the city."
Good-looking, fresh, apple-cheeked,
enthusiastic, rigid code.*

1	*AT RISE:*	The one-room apartment of MARGO RICHARDS who's
2		enjoyed a modest success in New York as an actress. Playbills,
3		play posters and eight-by-ten pictures are plastered all over the
4		walls. Furniture includes the usual combination living room-
5		kitchen setup. Door to the outside is on the left. The window
6		Upstage overlooks the New York skyline. The curtain opens on
7		the doorbell ringing furiously. MARGO is sitting at her card
8		table drinking her early morning coffee and reading "Variety."
9		She is dressed in a housecoat and she really is not quite up to
10		facing the day as yet.
11		
12		*(Doorbell rings again. MARGO rises, still holding coffee cup and*
13		*opens the door. CLIPPER MADISON stands there, the original*
14		*"Aw shucks" kid in jeans and sneakers. He flings out his arms.)*
15	CLIP:	**Good morning, Margo. Good morning, darling.** *(They*
16		*embrace and kiss.)*
17	MARGO:	**Good morning. Right on the stroke of ten. Clipper,**
18		**dear, aspiring New York actresses lucky enough to be in**
19		**a play — and that includes off-Broadway — sleep later in**
20		**the morning.**
21	CLIP:	**Then there was Jeff's party after the show. Keep you**
22		**up late last night?**
23	MARGO:	**Late enough.**
24	CLIP:	**Wish you didn't have these hours, Margo. At home,**
25		**back in Riderville, I used to be in bed at eleven. Every**
26		**night. New York's different naturally. And, of course,**
27		**stage people . . . Twelve's late enough though.**
28	MARGO:	**Don't worry about it. I'll go right back to sleep as**
29		**soon as you're gone. Coffee?**
30	CLIP:	**No, thanks. You wouldn't have any milk?**
31	MARGO:	*(She doesn't.)* **Oh, dear.**
32	CLIP:	**Doesn't matter. Not after I've told you my news. Look.**
33		*(Waves a letter at her. MARGO takes it.)* **A note from Miss**
34		**Sykes, Jeff Warren's secretary.**
35	MARGO:	*(Quickly reads note, throws it in the air in celebration.)*

1   Clip, no!
2   CLIP: Warren's reading my play. I'm not to sign with anyone
3   until I hear from him. Gosh, Margo, doesn't it take your
4   breath away?
5   MARGO: Clip, it's wonderful.
6   CLIP: If he only likes it well enough to produce it. If I could
7   only be sure — *(Snaps his fingers.)* Margo, you could do it.
8   Couldn't you?
9   MARGO: What?
10   CLIP: Give it a shove with Warren. The play. You're up at his
11   office a lot. Nothing obvious. Just say how much you like
12   it and there'd be a marvelous part in it for you, and if
13   ever there was a promising playwright, and —
14   MARGO: Not so fast, Clipper. Jeff's not one of those producers.
15   He doesn't work that way. Either he likes it or he doesn't.
16   CLIP: It wouldn't hurt if you'd —
17   MARGO: It's out of the question!
18   CLIP: Gee, honey, I'm sorry. Don't snap at me.
19   MARGO: I'm sorry too. Lack of sleep. But you can't use
20   friendship like that, Clip. I wouldn't before, and I —
21   CLIP: Before? What do you mean, before?
22   MARGO: Clip, don't pick up everything I say.
23   CLIP: All I asked was, what does before mean? Was there
24   something between you and Jeff?
25   MARGO: Would it matter?
26   CLIP: *(Slowly)* No.
27   MARGO: You don't sound very sure. And you're blushing
28   again.
29   CLIP: You said it so funny.
30   MARGO: Good heavens, what do you want?
31   CLIP: Gosh, why is our last morning going so sour? I thought
32   it —
33   MARGO: What was that?
34   CLIP: Let me get done. Our last morning just for a week.
35   MARGO: But — but —

1   CLIP: I didn't know she was coming. I —

2   MARGO: She? Who? Where? Would it be too much to ask —

3   CLIP: My mother.

4   MARGO: *(Sighs)* Oh.

5   CLIP: She's never been to New York.

6   MARGO: Really, Clip, there isn't one-half the suspense in
7   your play there is in you.

8   CLIP: I don't know why she has to come now. I told her —

9   MARGO: Clip, I'll be glad to help. We'll go sightseeing. All
10   three of us. Here's my chance to get to Grant's Tomb.

11   CLIP: That's just it.

12   MARGO: Wouldn't she like Grant's Tomb? We don't need to.

13   CLIP: Margo, this isn't meant for you. Please understand.
14   It's Mom's so old-fashioned. About actresses. She thinks
15   they're all —

16   MARGO: Hussies?

17   CLIP: Just about.

18   MARGO: But I'm not an actress, Clip. I'm the girl you love.

19   CLIP: She wouldn't understand. She'd be furious. A girl
20   sleeping all morning, racing about most of the night. I
21   couldn't offend her. It would really be better all around
22   if —

23   MARGO: I see.

24   CLIP: You're mad at me now, aren't you?

25   MARGO: I would be. If you meant that much to me.

26   CLIP: Margo, listen —

27   MARGO: I'm going to lose my temper in a minute, Clip. If you
28   left now, we might have a chance of staying friends.

29   CLIP: I thought I could break it to her — well, a little at a
30   time. I'm the baby of the family, and —

31   MARGO: The baby of the family! You underestimate yourself.
32   You're the baby of the age. I have a mother too, Sonny.
33   Does that surprise you? A mother from the country — just
34   like I am. Only we're not provincial and narrow and ashamed
35   of our friends. Do you think I'd mind bringing around the

1   man I love — if he swept streets, I'd be proud of him. He's

2   the one I'd be afraid to hurt. I don't know what you think

3   of me. I don't care what you think of me. Just take your

4   second-rate ideas on snobbery and clear out of my life.

5   Let me alone!

6   **CLIP:**   I guess this'll settle my play with Jeff Warren.

7   **MARGO:**   Did you hear me? Get out! Get out! *(CLIP extends his*

8   *hand. He's going to protest. Lets it drop. It's no use. He turns*

9   *swiftly and leaves. Door slams.)*

10   **MARGO:**   *(Furious)* **Oh.** *(She goes over and pours another cup of*

11   *coffee. She sits at table. She's going to drink it. She can't. She*

12   *breaks into tears, covers her face with her hands. Blackout.)*

13

14

15

16

17

18

19

20

21

22

23

24

25

26

27

28

29

30

31

32

33

34

35

A Name for Death

Cast of Characters

CAROL HAMPTON
Tense, nervous, about 35; plain; eager to please.

MICHAEL F. LARABEE
A powerfully built man of 67. Blind, he has won his way to the top through ruthlessness.

VIRGINIA LINTON
A good-looking woman of 28.

1   *AT RISE:*   The well-furnished living room and office of MICHAEL

2   LARABEE, wealthy, retired, blind bachelor. It is used as living

3   quarters, but since he still retains some business connections,

4   is used as an office as well. Sitting at desk typing is CAROL

5   HAMPTON.

6

7   **MICHAEL:**   *(Offstage)* **Carol! Carol!** *(She pulls sheet of paper from*

8   *typewriter, puts it on desk, then goes to door and opens it.)*

9   **CAROL:**   **Yes, Mr. Larabee.**

10   *(MICHAEL enters, wearing dark glasses. As he comes in, he*

11   *feels his wrist watch face, a watch for the blind with raised dots*

12   *on the numbers. The crystal has been snapped open. When he*

13   *learns the time, he will snap the crystal shut.)*

14   **CAROL:**   *(Cont.)* **Careful of the chair, Mr. Larabee.**

15   **MICHAEL:**   *(Ignoring this)* **Do you know what time it is?**

16   **CAROL:**   *(Looks at her watch.)* **Two o'clock.**

17   **MICHAEL:**   *(Angry)* **You know I only nap until one-thirty.**

18   **CAROL:**   **I'm sorry. I looked in the sun porch but you were**

19   **sleeping so soundly, I didn't have the heart to —**

20   **MICHAEL:**   **I don't pay you to watch me sleep. When I say one-**

21   **thirty, I mean one-thirty. Before this stupid thing**

22   **happened to my eyes, when I gave an order, it was carried**

23   **out.**

24   **CAROL:**   **Mr. Larabee, please. I — I don't know what to say.**

25   **MICHAEL:**   *(Furious)* **Then don't make a fool of me! When I**

26   **sold this business and came East, I may have retired, but**

27   **I didn't die, Miss Hampton. So, don't try to bury me!**

28   **CAROL:**   **I didn't think. I —**

29   **MICHAEL:**   **All right. What have we for this afternoon?**

30   **CAROL:**   **There's not much to be done, sir. And your niece said**

31   **she'd be here around two to take you for a ride . . . .**

32   **MICHAEL:**   **I said what have we got?**

33   **CAROL:**   **Just a few checks. They're all made out.** *(Hands him*

34   *checks.)*

35   **MICHAEL:**   *(As he takes them)* **And try to get it through your**

1		head that Mrs. Linton is not my niece. She's merely the
2		wife of my nephew. Did you put these through the check
3		writer so I can feel the numbers?
4	CAROL:	Yes, sir.
5	MICHAEL:	*(Runs his fingers over the first check.)* Seven-
6		hundred-and-forty dollars. For what?
7	CAROL:	Bates Plumbing and Supply. Repairs on your
8		apartment house in San Pedro.
9	MICHAEL:	Oh, yes. *(Signs check; picks up second.)* And this?
10	CAROL:	Pacific Power. Utility bill.
11	MICHAEL:	*(Reading)* Three-hundred-and-seventy-eight dollars
12		and sixty-three cents. It's up this month, isn't it?
13	CAROL:	About forty dollars.
14	MICHAEL:	*(Signs check.)* Too high.
15	CAROL:	The other's petty cash. A hundred-and-thirty-one
16		dollars.
17	MICHAEL:	For what?
18	CAROL:	*(Picks up list.)* Ten-fifty for the cleaners. Cook spent
19		seventy-eight-fifty on extra groceries she forgot when she
20		sent the order. Seventeen dollars to the drugstore. You
21		paid that out of the petty cash box yourself. And I bought
22		a roll of stamps, twenty-five dollars. It totals a hundred-
23		and-thirty-one.
24	MICHAEL:	*(Signing)* You've got to keep watch. When people
25		know you have a few dollars salted away, they try and
26		grab them. *(Hands her the signed checks.)* You'd try it too,
27		if I didn't use this check writer to protect myself.
28	CAROL:	That isn't fair, Mr. Larabee.
29	MICHAEL:	*(Laughing)* But I'd know if you were gyping me. I
30		don't think you would. As people go, you're pretty honest.
31	CAROL:	I've tried.... *(They turn as VIRGINIA LINTON is*
32		*heard calling.)*
33	VIRGINIA:	*(Offstage)* Uncle Mike.... *(VIRGINIA comes into*
34		*the room.)* Hi, Uncle Mike. It's Virginia.
35	CAROL:	Hello, Mrs. Linton.

1	**VIRGINIA:**	*(Impersonally)* **Hello.** *(To MICHAEL)* **I've come to**
2		**take you for a ride. It'll do you good.**
3	**MICHAEL:**	**I'm sorry, Virginia. I'm busy. When I want a ride,**
4		**I'll ask for one.**
5	**VIRGINIA:**	**Now, Mike. Don't be grouchy. We won't go for long.**
6	**MICHAEL:**	**We won't go at all. There's a real estate report I**
7		**want Carol to read to me . . . .**
8	**VIRGINIA:**	*(Cutting in)* **Mike, I don't know why you have to be**
9		**so tough and independent. Maybe people like to do things**
10		**for you. Did you ever think of that?**
11	**MICHAEL:**	**No, why should I? Virginia, I can't imagine**
12		**anything duller for you than riding me around in a car.**
13		**Unless, of course, your main interest is in my money.**
14	**VIRGINIA:**	**Aren't you wearing that joke a little thin?**
15	**MICHAEL:**	**I'm not joking. I told Bill when he married you he**
16		**did it on his own. Without my blessing.**
17	**VIRGINIA:**	**All right, you didn't get your own way for once in**
18		**your life. But that was three years ago. This is now. Come**
19		**on, it's a gorgeous afternoon.**
20	**MICHAEL:**	**Virginia, you're not stupid.**
21	**VIRGINIA:**	**Thanks.**
22	**MICHAEL:**	**Then why can't you get it through your head. *I***
23		***don't like you.*** *(She reacts.)* **You're nothing but a cheap**
24		**little fortune hunter who married Bill to get a lien on my**
25		**money. And now you're sniveling around to protect your**
26		**investment.**
27	**VIRGINIA:**	*(There is a pause; then she speaks quietly.)* **You know,**
28		**Mike, one of these days I may get fed up with you and**
29		**your temper.**
30	**MICHAEL:**	**I doubt it —**
31	**VIRGINIA:**	**I know it's not easy for you. I know you moved**
32		**East last year at Bill's suggestion, but just the same —**
33	**MICHAEL:**	*(He has scored.)* **What's the matter? Can't you stand**
34		**the truth?**
35	**VIRGINIA:**	**Oh, I can stand it all right. Even in front of Miss**

1　　　　　Hampton. But let me tell you —
2　　MICHAEL:　I'm not interested.
3　　VIRGINIA:　Well, you'll listen just the same. Maybe you don't
4　　　　　like me, but I married Bill, not you. And I wouldn't give
5　　　　　a hang if Bill were broke and you threw your precious
6　　　　　fortune in the river.
7　　MICHAEL:　That's easy to say. You know I'd never leave my
8　　　　　money to charity. And Bill's my only relative, so — *(He*
9　　　　　*shrugs.)*
10　VIRGINIA:　I mean it! *(She turns away.)* I'm sick and tired of all
11　　　　　this, Mike. I've tried, but you seem to enjoy making people
12　　　　　unhappy. I'm telling Bill tonight. *(She heads for the door.)*
13　　　　　Either it's our marriage, or —
14　　MICHAEL:　Where do you think you're going?
15　VIRGINIA:　Home.
16　MICHAEL:　Oh, no, not yet. I'm accepting your invitation.
17　　　　　We'll go for a ride — and you can tell Bill how patient
18　　　　　you were with me all afternoon.
19　VIRGINIA:　*(Takes deep breath.)* Mike, one of these days —
20　MICHAEL:　Stop babbling and hand me my cane. *(She does.)*
21　　　　　Carol —
22　　CAROL:　Yes, sir.
23　MICHAEL:　See that you stay until five. I'll call then — to check.
24　　CAROL:　Yes, sir. Have a nice ride.
25　MICHAEL:　*(Chuckling)* Oh, we will.
26　　CAROL:　Bye.
27　VIRGINIA:　*(As they leave)* Want to take my arm?
28　MICHAEL:　I can manage for myself. *(They exit.)*
29　　　　　*(CAROL runs to window to watch them go. As soon as she is*
30　　　　　*sure, her expression changes, and she picks up checks MICHAEL*
31　　　　　*has signed and very deliberately tears them up, then puts them*
32　　　　　*in ashtray and burns them. While they are burning, she opens*
33　　　　　*drawer, takes out a new set of checks which she glances over. As*
34　　　　　*she looks, she smiles, then sits down to sign the checks with*
35　　　　　*MICHAEL's signature. Blackout.)*

ABOUT THE AUTHOR

Sigmund Stoler, born and raised on the eastern coast, has two successful work careers to his credit — writer and psychologist.

His "New York period," the fifties and early sixties, included not only his script writing for radio and television, but he also published over two hundred and fifty short stories, innumerable articles, had representative work in a series of one-act play anthologies, and saw two of his short stories included in *True Story's* anthology of the fourteen best stories that magazine ever published.

He was awarded a master of arts degree from Bucknell University in 1963, and three years later, began work as a psychologist at an institution for the mentally retarded. In 1971, he opened his first psychiatric out-patient clinic in Sunbury, Pennsylvania. One clinic eventually grew to four, employing twenty-five persons. Now, the writer-psychologist divides his time between both his vocations.

For the country's bicentennial, 1976, he and the late Lorne Greene did a record album together, *Pennsylvania, the Keystone State.* More recently, he continues writing for the magazine markets and working on two novels. He is presently rewriting one of them, *Borderline,* that he plans to bring out early in 1990.

In his spare time, he and his wife, Betty, a registered nurse, enjoy bridge (even as partners), the theatre, movies, television, golf, walking, and their French poodle, Alfie. The Stolers live off a golf course in central Pennsylvania.

ORDER FORM

mp™ **MERIWETHER PUBLISHING LTD.**
P.O. BOX 7710
COLORADO SPRINGS, CO 80933
TELEPHONE: (719) 594-4422

Please send me the following books:

_____**TV Scenes for Actors #TT-B137**   **$14.95**
by Sigmund A. Stoler
Selected short scenes from the Golden Age of TV Drama

_____**Encore! More Winning Monologs for Young $7.95
Actors #TT-B144**
by Peg Kehret
More honest-to-life monologs for young actors

_____**Winning Monologs for Young Actors #TT-B127 $7.95**
by Peg Kehret
Honest-to-life monologs for young actors

_____**Two Character Plays for Student Actors #TT-B174 $7.95**
by Robert Mauro
A collection of 15 one-act plays

_____**Original Audition Scenes for Actors #TT-B129 $9.95**
by Garry Michael Kluger
A book of professional-level dialogs and monologs

_____**57 Original Auditions for Actors #TT-B181 $6.95**
by Eddie Lawrence
A workbook of monologs for actors

_____**Theatre Games for Young Performers #TT-B188 $7.95**
by Maria C. Novelly
Improvisations and exercises for developing acting skills

*I understand that I may return any book
for a full refund if not satisfied.*

NAME: _____

ORGANIZATION NAME: _____

ADDRESS: _____

CITY: _____ STATE: _____ ZIP:_____

PHONE: _____

☐ **Check Enclosed**
☐ **Visa or Master Card #**_____

Signature: _____
(required for Visa/Mastercard orders)

COLORADO RESIDENTS: Please add 3% sales tax.
SHIPPING: Include $1.50 for the first book and 50¢ for each additional book ordered.

☐ *Please send me a copy of your complete catalog of books or plays.*